1201386 656 387 BROOK

Please renew/return this item by the last date shown.

So that your telephone call is charged at local rate, please call the numbers as set out below:

	From Area codes 01923 or 0208:	From the rest of Herts:
Renewals:	01923 471373	01438 737373
Enquiries:	01923 471333	01438 737333
Minicom:	01923 471599	01438 737599

L32b

L.32

TURMOIL

Turmoil, a squat powerful giant waits on station

TURMOIL

EWART BROOKES

WITH 26 PHOTOGRAPHS

Sleepe after toil, port after stormy seas,
Ease after warre, doth greatly please.

JARROLDS *Publishers* (LONDON) LTD
FOUNDED IN 1770

LIST OF ILLUSTRATIONS

AUTHOR'S NOTE

WHEN first it was suggested to me that I should write a book on the tug *Turmoil* I considered the project with a considerable degree of diffidence.

From experience I knew that quite often a subject which will produce sufficient material for a long article, or even a series of articles, dwindles off to a fine and unsubstantial taper when drawn out to the length of a reasonably long book.

For that to happen in execution would be unfair to both subject and to the reader.

I knew, of course, that there was a fair amount of material about regarding *Turmoil*, particularly on her gallant, if unavailing, attempt to rescue the American freighter *Flying Enterprise* in late December 1951 and early January 1952. And one or two other incidents.

But turning that material into a book would be another matter.

I think I was swayed, in the main, towards accepting the task by two factors.

Here they are in their order.

As the project was being discussed and was still in an extremely fluid state *Turmoil* again came into the news last December by her Homeric rescue of half of the tanker *World Concord* in that deadly stretch of water from the southern end of the Irish Sea to the Clyde precincts.

I know those waters in their every mood. I have sailed over them in yachts, in merchant ships and in command of H.M. ships, and please believe me when I say that it is no place to be with trouble on your hands. And *Turmoil* had trouble on her hands that trip.

I listen to the weather forecasts with one eye on the effect of it on the sea—although I have, to use a seaman's phrase, "swallowed the anchor". As we talked over the pros and cons of doing a book on her *Turmoil* was battling through a gale which, with that fiendish glee it seems to possess, was swinging about and coming anywhere from the south-east to the south-west and was swinging back again in the proverbial twinkling of an eye.

Turmoil succeeded, and when I read the short communication in Lloyd's *Shipping Intelligence* that she had reached Holy Loch with her half-ship I felt that there was more in that story than was told. There was.

I agreed to explore the possibilities. And as I explored, the broader picture of deep-sea rescue and towage unfolded itself before me and the fascination grew . . . and grew.

The names of other famous tugs began to appear in my growing accumulation of notes. Names like *Bustler, Dexterous, Englishman, Salveda, Rumania,* the Metal Industries *Metindas,* those wonderful Dutch tugs the *Maas,* the *Zwarte Zee,* the *Oost Zee,* the *Oceaan* and the French tugs, the *Abeilles.*

Finally I realized that far from there being not enough material there was too much and the task would be one of selection and reluctant rejection—for the time being!

I had to keep in mind that my story was to be mainly around *Turmoil,* but any story about her would inevitably bring to mind some other story about some other tug.

So it went and so it is.

Let *Turmoil* be the representative of a type of ship sailed by a type of seamen who concede nothing in quality of seamanship to any other branch in the seagoing world, even of any other generation. They go unsung, often unhonoured, never glamorized.

That was the first factor; the unceasing fascination anything to do with ships and the sea has for me, plus the professional knowledge that there was material available.

The second factor was that during the war I had seen rescue tugs operate.

But what of their peace-time tasks?

I had seen them go about their task of mercy in that cockpit, the Dover Straits. I had watched them go out to ships which were, through the evils of war, in that state described by Maeterlinck as a state of "nameless, hopeless distress".

Harassed by bombs, machine-gun fire and shells, and working over minefields—because stricken ships did not keep to the narrow, swept channels—they went ahead more or less calmly, but with unquestioned celerity and skill, on their rescue job.

I had seen them, too, function in convoys in darker and colder waters farther north, had watched them slam through all the Pentland Firth could do—and that was plenty—and had watched them drop astern—with mixed emotions as they played nurse, comforter and saviour to some ship which had been hit in convoy and compelled to drop out of the deadly battle we were then fighting.

Yet, I had never seen one close-to except for a brief period, later in the war, when I lay alongside a deep-sea tug called the *Sea Giant*. She was, to within a few feet, as long as the fighting ship I commanded. But her engines were more than four times as powerful. Whereas we had scarcely enough room to swing a very short cat (the nine-thonged variety, not the milk-drinking species) on our decks, she had enough room on her towing deck to hold a dance with a fair-sized band to accompany it.

As I looked at her I visualized activity, far removed from dancing, which would go on when she had a job.

She went her way, I went mine, but thinking of rescue tugs once more brought her to mind, and, curiously enough, in searching for material I met the man who was responsible for bringing her over the Atlantic from her peaceful pursuits to a field of war.

I can drape myself over a bridge, or a quay wall, and look at ships for hours. Whether they be coasters with coal from the Tyne to London, or Baltic traders, their decks high with timber, or ships from the River Plate with grain, or loaded with that sullen cargo, iron ore, I can recapture the scenes on their decks as they lay alongside quay walls many sea miles away.

But tugs, whether they be small, busy harbour tugs or powerful deep-sea towing tugs, are—or were—closed books to me.

My tentative exploration of the possibilities became a deeply rooted interest and a fascinating picture lay before me when I had completed the exploration.

Finally I capitulated, and here is the story of *Turmoil*, with amplyifying accounts of other tugs on other jobs.

To tell the whole story of deep-sea towage would take a book for each of the tugs—full books at that.

Each would be packed with incident, with adventure, with stories of selfless devotion to duty, with stories of superb seamanship, either on rescue or tow, and would take a lifetime to write.

When next you read that a rescue tug has gone out to save a stricken ship, or possibly read, briefly, that a tug has taken in tow an unwieldy dredger or elevator for some far corner of the world, then you will know, I hope, after reading this book, that the job is being done by tugmen—*real* seamen.

July, 1955.   E. B.

CHAPTER ONE

FOR more than ten days the Atlantic has raved and stormed. From the American seaboard to Finisterre, Ushant, Land's End, Fastnet, Old Head of Kinsale, The Smalls, The Mull of Kintyre, the Hebrides to Cape Wrath and the Butt of Lewis, towering, roaring lethal seas have hammered themselves into futile creaming spray.

West of a line drawn through those navigational focal points, and east of the American seaboard, a couple of hundred, or more, ships are battling with the full might of a succession of late autumn gales.

The mighty "Queens", *Elizabeth* and *Mary*, exquisitely handled with fingertip control, and speed adjusted to a hair's-breadth nicety, have slashed through with only minor damage to their structure, a slightly disrupted time-table, thankfully laconic reports from weary-eyed captains—and passengers with fearsome tales to garnish many a future dinner-table.

North of them rust-streaked, high-bowed trawlers, with little more freeboard than a wet matchstick, dodge and lie hove-to with grim Rockall as their datum point, waiting for a slight easing of the gale before shooting their trawls again, with their skippers becoming more irascible as gale succeeds gale and bunkers get lower with fish holds not half full.

Between those two extremes, threaded like beads on an invisible string, ships of a dozen nationalities, of half a hundred firms, are battling with those same gales, pointing either west or east from Ambrose Light, the first portal into the United States.

Some are hove-to, engines turning at less than half speed, hulls moaning and creaking as they roll and pitch. Others, confidently pitting the cunning of their designers and the power of their engines (plus the knowledge that a day lost is

less profit on ledgers in narrow St. Mary Axe, E.C.) adjust
their engine speeds and creep forward five miles onward, two
sideways. And unceasingly the Atlantic hammers and raves,
seeking a victim, a ship with a weakness, a ship where tired
men, closing eyes for the length of two deep breaths, will
lower their guards.

Thunderous, roaring white-crested seas, half a mile or
more apart, their tips whipped into lashing battle plumes of
hail-like spray, race along the howling wind that provides the
martial music. Between the seas dark, white speckled hollows,
momentarily and strangely quiet, offer a deceptive and deadly
respite. A wrong move of the wheel, too great a reduction of
engine revolutions, in one of those death valleys and a ship
would be beam-on to the next mountain of water, would be
engulfed and the triumphant martial wind music would have
an undertone of requiem.

Through it all an almost unceasing thin thread of radio is
sewn into the fabric. A ship, late and behind schedule, is
ordered to another port, a cargo of grain is switched from
Avonmouth to Rotterdam while the ship carrying it is still
fighting her way across. Business tycoons on the liners flood
the ether with long messages which increase or decrease the
prices of stocks and shares. A sleek, curved film star (or her
publicity agent) flatly denies, or equally dogmatically confirms,
at length, the latest story of one of her innumerable marriages
or divorces.

Then suddenly, dramatically, as if somebody had shut a
door on it all, there is silence but for a hesitant signal, so weak
at times that listeners have to strain for it.

A ship is in trouble.

The attenuated, almost bat-like piping of the stricken ship
is eventually deciphered and to the world goes out a message:

"A Lloyd's message from Land's End Radio dated Nov. 2
states:

"Following received from British steamer *Galaxy* 8.45
p.m. G.M.T. Position 50.40 North long. 20.55 West. Cargo

shifted, ship has 20 degree list, being swept by heavy seas, fires extinguished, lifeboats smashed, some casualties."

The Atlantic has found a victim.

The mountainous seas rave and claw, pile over the wallow-ing ship, rage and storm as she rises sluggishly from succeeding attacks and the wind reaches a fiendish howl.

On a dozen ships water drips from oilskin hats as masters and mates study charts, work out their proximity, realize the impossibility of being able to reach her and render help, look each other straight in the eyes and turn to a scowling scrutiny of the seas with a breathed prayer on their lips: "There, but for the grace of God, go I."

Nearer to her a long, lean tanker alters course, double banks look-outs, prepares to spill oil by the ton over the sea, if they find her, so that she will have at least a slim fighting chance.

A freighter increases speed by a couple of knots. A risk, but one to be taken while master and mate search in their minds for rusted details of boat management in heavy seas and ponder the problem of getting a tow across if it is humanly possible.

In the meantime the story has elaborated from the hesitant piping of *Galaxy's* auxiliary radio set.

Four days earlier the wind had ripped away a hatch cover over number two hold. With the restraining stout canvas gone, despite herculean efforts on the part of the chief officer, bos'n and several seamen, some of the hatchboards had gone over-board. Water had got into the hold. Her pitching and rolling had developed a sullen jerk. In the early hours of the morning a mightier sea than the others had rolled her over on to her beam ends. For long agonizing seconds she had stayed there, had swung beam-on to the seas, water had poured into every aperture, a cloud of steam had signalled the defeat of the fires.

Then, to a ship rolling uneasily at Cobh, on the south coast of Ireland, had come some short, terse messages.

Her powerful Diesel engines had throbbed and hummed into life. Almost before she cleared Roche's Point, the mouth of the harbour, her captain had studied the chart of the area, had drawn an optimistic circle on it, a ring round 50.40 North, 20.55 West.

As she reached the open sea a creaming, rolling sea, with all the might of the Atlantic, had reared up at her, as if recognizing a mercy-bent saviour for the stricken ship farther west.

But the broad, sharply rising bow of the ship had disdainfully met it, climbed over it, leaving it broken behind it, and prepared for the next . . . and the next.

For this was a ship built to save, designed to meet all that the oceans could produce, and survive it.

A deep sea rescue tug.

When men had bent over drawing-boards limning in her first lines they had drawn heavily on the Bank of Experience, had drawn on a credit account first established when man had timorously sat astride a log and had ridden down a placid stream, had learned to use his weight to guide it, had learned to sit well back to give the front of the log a rise to climb above the water, had learned that with a piece of wood in his hands he could make it alter direction, with a piece of skin held aloft he could make the wind help.

Through the centuries men had added to the account until the day came when this ship, this rescue tug, all thousand tons of her, had slipped smoothly down the slipway, the ultimate in tugs.

And to her came a man to be her captain, from a frightened boy of twelve on a creaking fishing smack, through youth and early manhood, through wars and peace, calm and gales; he, too, had added to his Bank of Experience until he stood, peerless, legs widely astride, he and his ship a superb combination which stood for skill, and mercy.

Carefully, a few revolutions at a time, her captain increases speed until he has judged, with exquisite judgment, that his ship is giving of her best. At a speed which would be suicidal for a heavy freighter she slams powerfully into the gale. Time is vital, time is money—time means lives.

Signal follows signal. *Galaxy's* thin voice is seldom heard; she is saving her batteries. The tanker and freighter report they cannot yet see her nor the occasional rockets she is firing. Visibility is less than half a mile and darkness is hanging on to an already over-long reign.

The world watches, through the terse signals, the fight to save the ship. But first she must be found.

On the squat bridge of the tug her captain works out a problem. A problem which in turn is made up of a whole series of smaller complicated fragments as a jigsaw puzzle is made, with the puzzle not complete until the last piece, the sighting of the stricken ship, drops into place.

A powerful finger hovers over the last reported position of *Galaxy*. Was that by dead reckoning? Had her captain, bereft of sunsights for days, estimated that position by distance run, estimating the set of the wind, the force of the current, estimating errors of commission and omission by tired men at the wheel? Had he cautiously over-estimated his position knowing he might shortly make a landfall off Old Head of Kinsale?

Or had he under-estimated power and weight of wind and tide, the occasional extra thrust as she raced down the steep side of a sea?

Was he north and east of his estimated position? Or was he south and west of it?

The short, powerful fingers tap a tattoo on the large-scale chart as the tug's captain weighs everything in the balance.

Shall he steam to the last reported position, he, too, working on estimated distance run, judging the force of wind, tide and sea? Shall he start his search from there? Or . . . the fingers cease their tattoo. Some curious sixth sense comes to his aid. Were he asked to describe it he would call it a hunch, and would be wrong. The tapping fingers cease, the broad hand drops flat on the chart, firmly, decisively. He has drawn on his account.

He studies the swinging compass for a few seconds, tilts a chin upwards and watches the seas roaring out of the darkness.

B

"Bring her to South 70 West . . . don't let her go anything to South of that."

"Sou' 70 West, sir. Nothing to suth'ard."

She slams through the grey, wild dawn, on through the short day until towards evening, when fading light starts to fight a reluctant rearguard action against encroaching blackness and feelings become tense.

Nobody had found *Galaxy*, two faint signals had come from her, the list was increasing, the seas were sweeping her bodily, the crew were sheltering amidships.

Even the tug seems to sense that the next few hours will be vital.

On the crest of each sea she poises for a long moment, bluff bow held upwards as a hound lifts its head for a moment from the scent.

Visibility is down to half a mile, the distance between two bus stops.

The square, powerful hands have never shown a trace of falter, not a tap of indecision as they grip the rail, or the edge of the chart table.

Midnight creeps on inexorably.

"Rockets fine on the starboard bow."

A curving thread of light climbs upwards, bursts into an incandescent glow for a moment, a head bends over a compass, takes a swift bearing before the light dies.

"Found her!" Found her in the dark of the night.

And soon the world knows that the tug has located the stricken ship.

Then the epic starts. Finding her was the beginning.

As the tug closes in his searchlight stabs across the water and the tug captain studies the helpless vessel. At times only her bridge shows above water, then she rises in a labouring, shuddering heave. Sea cascades from her decks, she gives a curious lurch to upright, then wallows down again as wave after wave slams aboard breaking into white water against the deck-houses.

The captain of the tug has no committee of Ways and Means to consult. He has to make decisions which are final and binding with the seal of death for forty men or more set on such decision if he is wrong.

A few hundred feet separate the ships, the gap a ribbon of glowing green white from the searchlight.

She still has a reserve of buoyancy; she could ride the sea if she could be brought round head or stern to it. So, with oil spilling out over the water from the tug to slick down the sea, the tug captain edges closer.

At that range they have managed to make talk with *Galaxy's* fading radio. *Galaxy's* crew is exhausted, hungry, and fear is but a gulp away deep down in their throats.

"She won't last the night at the rate she is being beaten. I'm going to pass the tow."

The tug captain knows his officers and crew, all with accounts in the same Bank of Experience, each posted to do a part, whether it be merely to twist a throttle, throw a line, nurse a spinning wheel or man-handle a tow line half as thick as a man's body.

And this is where the tug captain's account is once more drawn upon.

He knows that while he can get a line across to the *Galaxy*, her crew, wet, afraid, exhausted, would be physically incapable of hauling across by hand the heavier tow.

The oil has momentarily tamed the awe-inspiring fury of the sea; no longer does it smash savagely over all the ship except the bridge. The *Galaxy's* forecastle head, although almost constantly awash, is livable.

The tug captain passes his instructions to the ship. An affirmative answer comes back A rocket snakes through the air carrying with it a light line; it drops cleanly, truly across the *Galaxy's* bridge and clutching hands seize it. A small knot of resolute men battle through chest-high water along her flooded fore-deck, clamber up on to her forecastle, hands clenched tightly round the light line. They start to haul. What they pull aboard is a slightly heavier endless line. Once that is aboard the tug does the rest. The endless line travels back to her, a heavier line, and ultimately the thick tow with heavy shackles complete arrives on the *Galaxy* having demanded no physical effort from her weary men.

With almost a sob of relief they secure it, their slim chance of life.

The tug slowly, craftily takes the strain and moves ahead into the darkness.

Out of the night looms the tanker.

"Can I help?"

Help she can. The tug can no longer offer an oil slick so, until she has them both balanced and moving, the tanker contributes her quota, spreading a fluid as timeless and as ageless as the sea itself.

At last the tug has her moving. It is a slow and painful progress with disaster waiting just in the wings, waiting for a slip or a mistake to be its cue to leap in and again take the centre of the stage.

Have you ever stood and watched a boy fly a kite?

Have you watched the kite at the end of the curved and soaring line? Have you watched it hold there, docile and controlled? Have you seen the kite suddenly swerve away in a series of breath-taking dives first to one side, then the other, with the line becoming bar-tight?

And have you seen the tortured line suddenly snap and the kite wallow away fluttering to minor disaster?

Translate that to a horizontal plane and you have a picture of the problem facing the tug captain for every second he has the ship in tow. He has to play it like a large salmon. For a time the two ships, towed and towing, fit into the metronomic measure of the towering seas and deep foam-flecked valleys.

Then suddenly the towed ship takes a sheer off to one side. She slips down the steep of a sea at an angle, like the kite swoops down; the tow becomes momentarily bar-tight, she is out on the quarter of the tug instead of being astern and that

disaster-laden movement can start in a period of three long
breaths.

The tug is equipped with a magnificent winch designed to
give and take almost extravagant variations of strain, and it
does, but that sheer off to the quarter demands seamanship of
a high and peculiar quality.

If the boy with the kite is wise he gives line, perhaps walks
a few paces to spill the strain until he has his soaring captive
balanced and steady.

The tug captain does the same, moving over towards his
tow; the strain relaxes and she drops dutifully astern.

And this goes on for hour after hour through the darkness.

The tanker, reassured, has gone on her way. They are alone.
Somewhere off to port side are the gaunt cliffs of south-west
Ireland. In an emergency Cork harbour would do, but the tug
captain is now confident that he can tow the *Galaxy* anywhere
that is wanted short of the Gates of Hell itself—and he has
been towing her FROM them for hours.

A snarling, grey dawn creeps upwards and the tug captain,
the lines deep on his face, lifts his binoculars for a first scrutiny
of his charge.

He nudges his Chief Officer, who is keeping vigil with him.

"Do you see what I see?"

A wisp of smoke is rising from the *Galaxy's* cook's galley,
a wisp which is whipped away almost as soon as it is born.

The Chief Officer grins.

"Maybe half a dozen eggs and a couple or three rashers a
man . . . saloon feeding for the lot."

"And hot coffee, plenty of it."

The Chief Officer, with recollections of his own days on
merchant ships, hazards another guess.

"And the Old Man opening up a few bottles with large
tots for the bunch that worked the tow aboard—one of them
being the Mate, of course."

The tug master adds to the lines on his face with a crinkly
smile.

"Maybe." He cocks an eye at the sea, at the sky, at the obstinately low barometer. "I'll be happier when I get her round the corner. There's still some dirt to come."

All day they plod along, counteracting the sudden and unpredictable swoops and swerves, alone on the grey sea.

Towards evening course is altered. Inshore, where they cannot see it, is Conigberg Light; they are moving into the Irish Sea, the seas are steeper, not so powerful, but snappily vicious, with more of them in a given period.

"She's sitting nicely now. I'm going to get my head down."

No need for the captain to order a call if there is an emergency. He knows he will get it. And get it he does.

A snarling squall of furious wind and stinging rain hits them with a bang. *Galaxy* disappears into the grey-black screen.

"Tow's parted!"

No panic. No rushing about with a stream of lurid oaths garnishing a machine-gun fire of orders.

Just one question and one order.

"Got her on radar?"

"Yes, sir."

"Stand by to pass tow."

Again an epic on its own. Nudging in by radar until she is visible, again wallowing on her beam ends. Again a light line is passed, then a heavier one snakes aboard the *Galaxy*; once again the heavy tow is secured.

Three times that happens and ironically each time it happens in the darkness.

Finally out of the murk South Stack light looms, the radio is busy, then the Bar Light, hostess to all ships entering the Mersey.

Smaller, squat tugs, past-masters in the art of intricate movement in restricted areas, wait like ample nurses. The deep sea tug hands over and as she does a yellow sun stabs through, touches a cloud with gold, lights up the group of ships as if with a spotlight. The clouds are chased away. Away inshore the small tugs nudge and coax at *Galaxy's* unwieldy bulk.

Our tug swings away, a boil of white under her stern.

"Orders are Milford Haven. A straight tow to Avonmouth. That tanker which had the fire a few weeks ago."

The telegraph jangles.

An older member of the crew leans over the rail, talking to the latest and youngest to join.

"Did you see that tall building, the one with the birds on it?"

The youngster is not certain but says he did.

"Royal Liver building, that. And whenever a salvage tug loses a tow the birds flap their wings."

"They're not real. Their wings can't flap."

"That's what I mean."

The youngster ponders deeply and uncertainly as the tug slips through the water at a steady fourteen knots, oblivious that her name is on the front pages of newspapers over half the world.

In his berth the captain lies, arms folded, eyes closed, chest rising and falling. He is making up arrears of sleep. Who knows, another S.O.S. might scream through the ether? So sleep when it is possible.

His tug thrusts contemptuously through the sullen and frustrated sea, her powerful bow parting it into harmless white spray, her broad, low stern riding over it with ease.

Such a tug could be *Turmoil*.

CHAPTER TWO

THE previous chapter is a composite story of rescue, the elements of any of half a dozen epics compressed into one to give a picture of the work done by the specialized deep sea tugs which keep a twenty-four hour ceaseless watch.

The popular picture of them lying at anchor, or rising and falling uneasily against a quay wall in some craftily chosen port, waiting only for a breathless distress call is far removed from the true version.

Turmoil, like other deep-sea tugs, works for a living at the mundane business of towing. At the flick of a pen at the foot of a contract tugs of her class are prepared to journey across the world on a tow, and they are completely equipped to do so.

Another popular conception of a tug is almost inevitably founded on seeing those smaller versions which work in the main estuaries and docks round the coast. Of course they, in their place, are masters of the art of manœuvre in close places. Fascinating hours can be spent watching small tugs swing a string of unwieldy barges down and across tide to place them with meticulous precision against a ship or wharf in the Thames.

Or when some deep-laden freighters or liners timorously enter close waters they bustle up to them, spin in their own length and either take a line from bow or stern or put their heavily padded stem against them and resolutely urge them alongside the quay with a judicious, firm push.

Every dock and trading estuary has them, even the humble canals, and most people must have pondered and marvelled at the power they can produce, at their ability to move purposefully in little more than their own length.

When it comes to studying the picture of *Turmoil* and her sister tugs and the work they do, then the vista alters.

Turmoil displaces 1,118 tons, is 1,630 tons when fully loaded. She is 205 feet long, 41 feet broad in the beam at the maximum point, draws more than 17 feet of water and her 4,000 B.H.P. Atlas Polar Diesel engines can drive her along at 16 knots— nearly 20 miles an hour, and what is more important, can develop towing powers to move and control almost any ship afloat even if that ship be half full of water.

She takes aboard 400 tons of fuel oil and when that is aboard she has a cruising range of 17,000 miles.

Her bridge is equipped with every navigational device. She has radar, echo sounding and direction finding radio as well as the normal and latest types of radios.

To run this towing colossus takes a crew of 27, and at a given moment, without flurry or fuss each man has his appointed task and does it, fitting into the over-all plan snugly, competently, with supreme confidence in the captain.

Turmoil is one of a class built during the war as rescue tugs, sailing at the tail of a convoy ready to take in tow any ship bombed or torpedoed. It was a task which evoked unceasing admiration from those on the escorting ships.

A convoy as a whole did have some measure of protection from U-boats. The destroyer, frigates and corvettes circling the herd could, and did, hit back.

But a convoy could not be slowed down for a stricken ship. She had to be left behind, alone, until the rescue tug could take her in tow.

There were many poignant moments in convoy when the broad array of ships steamed on avoiding the victim, watched her drop astern into the night, the only, and slim, comfort being the knowledge that somewhere back in that darkness was a ship equipped to take her in tow, equipped to battle with all the Western ocean could offer and prepared to fling down the gauntlet and tilt against a detached U-boat seeking an easy victim.

It always brought a thrill of pride and admiration to commanding officers of warships when they were sent out to escort in a rescue tug and its charge. In the murk off the Butt of Lewis, or Gibraltar, or off Iceland, a rendezvous would be briefly arranged. Estimated positions of U-boats would be studied and off would race the frigate or corvette or, more often, the asdic trawler, her stern bristling with depth charges.

Binoculars would ceaselessly sweep the sea ahead, radar would search the surface, asdic would ping below. Then, looming up through the grey, spindrift-laden day, would come the tug. Bow cocked up jauntily, broad stern squatting down and astern of her, the tow sagging into the water, would be the torpedoed ship, in her side a ragged hole the size of a house; perhaps her bridge would be twisted and shattered.

Alone they had made it.

There is one classic story of the rescue tug at the tail end of a convoy in northern, snow- and gale-swept waters which searched for and found a torpedoed merchantman.

Then for nearly a week there was silence, a silence which provided the framework for tragic conjecture that she and her charge had been caught by the battered, angry remnant of a U-boat pack and had been sunk. Until one grey-black morning a patrol trawler challenged by Aldis light a ship which loomed up out of the murk.

It was the rescue tug, her tow wallowing and charging astern, decks awash, wearied in spirit and body, but still alive.

"Challenge made." "Challenge answered."

A few more terse signals as the trawler steamed round the two in a protective circle, her probing asdic searching the waters.

In an afterthought the tug's Aldis light blinked again.

"A few miles astern there is a German plane in the drink. A Dornier, I think."

"Good old Coastal Command," thought the commanding officer of the trawler, "or maybe some racing destroyer on special mission bound."

"How far? And who shot it down?"

"We did."

With an antiquated 4-inch gun and two Oerlikon machine-guns the rescue tug had accepted the challenge from the skies and turned her flaming reply into brief but final victory. And went on her way, if not rejoicing at least confident.

The weather broke down badly. For two days the three ships fought it, finally reaching the quieter waters of the Minches. As they entered, the trawler, preparing to swing off to her lawful occasions, asked: "Anything I can do for you?"

Back came the signal:

"Yes, settle an argument. What year did Cardiff City win the Cup?"

Gales? Important, no doubt. Enemy submarines and air-craft? Threatening and dangerous, no doubt. But what endless argument in the tug's mess deck was to be settled by the answer to that one vital question?

THAT was important.

Unfortunately, when war broke out this country found itself woefully short of tugs of the calibre capable of taking the sea in any weather, remaining with a convoy until ships were hit, taking one of them in tow and bringing her back to harbour.

There were a few and they were grossly overworked. And some of them fell victims to the German bombs and torpedoes.

It was the same soul-wearying story which coloured the war even until it was more than half way through its span.

Too few ships for far too many jobs.

Large and powerful trawlers, which were urgently wanted for minesweeping, patrol and convoy, were pressed into service as rescue craft.

They did their best, but they had their limitations. Ships, which in the latter stages of the war would have presented no more than normal problems, went down because deep sea tugs were not available.

It is no exaggeration to say that masters and crews of hard-pressed merchant ships drew almost as much comfort from the knowledge that a deep-sea tug, sometimes two, were

tucked in astern of the convoy as they did from the presence of
a couple of extra corvettes and frigates.

They knew that if disaster placed them at the end of a long
white streak—a torpedo track—provided they did not sink
immediately, resolute and skilful help was available.

But before that day could arrive much thought and midnight oil was used up at conferences at the Admiralty.

Improvisation was not enough. It was a major problem
and the only answer was "tugs".

Like other problems of the war, there were men with the
knowledge to provide the answer and to them the Admiralty
turned.

Even today, because of the nature of their work they
command anonymity—and anonymous they must remain.

As in every other kind of business snags continually arise
in towage and salvage, arise and have to be met and demolished. So grows experience. If these experts had anything
at all they had that.

They had handled all the complexities of deep sea towing
and salvage for a number of years. They knew the problems
involved; they knew tugs, they knew men. They also realized
to the full what the result would be of the tragic scarcity of
deep sea tugs in the free waters of the world.

There were the men; give them the tools and let them get on
with the job, the Admiralty decided.

The short answer, to these men, was build. But every
yard in the country was working the clock round building
merchant ships to replace the almost astronomical losses at
sea, or were engaged in constructing warships of which the
losses were nearly as high in proportion.

By contacts known to them they heard that the Americans
were willing to let us have tugs.

Right! Then they must go to America and find the tugs.

They found, as indeed they had expected to find, that
no ready solution lay on the American seaboard.

To men who for nearly half a century had lived deep sea

tugs and salvage the potentialities of nearly every deep sea tug in the world was known to them as possible rivals.

But they hoped that somewhere in the ports on America's seaboards they would find some tugs which would serve, which would be an extension of our pitiful improvisation until we could tackle the problem in the only adequate way he knew, and that was "to build".

They were offered tugs, it was true, with a wealth of enthusiasm by the Americans who had but a glimmering of the problem involved.

Most of you will remember that film classic *Tug Boat Annie* and the decrepit wooden slab-sided tug which was almost the co-star in the film.

Many hundred miles were travelled to see such ships only to dismiss them with little more than a glance.

They couldn't have stood a few hours' hammering in the Channel, never mind a ten days' winter North Atlantic passage.

To their eternal credit they did get some tugs, more than a dozen, and there are people who today wonder where they got them, and how, but get them they did.

To them, with a clear-cut conception of what was wanted, and the immensity of the problem involved, it loomed as a partial failure, but from a harassed Admiralty they received gracious and well-earned thanks.

These they brushed aside. The problem still remained a PROBLEM and one to which they wanted to find an answer.

At that time a small tug there was working every hour of every day and in her were embodied the essentials of the type of tug which would fill the bill of requirements for a rescue tug.

When officials with but a faint idea of what deep-sea towage and rescue work involved wanted to sit back with a "something-attempted-something-done" attitude they suddenly found themselves facing a small body of men who were interested in only one thing, Tugs, powerful tugs which could keep the sea in any weather. Those tugs they were determined to obtain. And the only way was to BUILD. It became a litany with them—an emphatic chorus.

There were others who would argue and fight for more aircraft, fight for more tanks, more guns, more men, more destroyers, more corvettes, more merchant ships.

More power to their elbows, but rescue tugs were wanted; they had given them the job. So . . .

The answer was short and to the point.

BUILD.

Pouted lips and precedent-bound officials demurred.

Building would mean planning. Naval architects would have to crouch over drawing-boards and . . . and . . . and . . .

One objection after another was raised, to be demolished by men who knew, lived and breathed tugs.

A passing thought might arise here. Before the war started there were tugs in plenty shared mainly by the three big maritime nations of Europe—England, France and Holland.

All three had maintained big rescue tugs on stations the length of the Eastern Atlantic seaboard and when war broke out their work was intensified and some extra stations were allocated.

Those tugs had to remain there at focal points, being much too valuable, too vital in fact to switch to convoy work.

That was the problem, finding rescue tugs which could sail with convoys and could augment the tugs on set stations.

The full impact was not felt until after the fall of France, until after Holland had been overrun and until Dunkirk had become a bitter memory.

The battle of the Atlantic was yet to be joined to the degree of savage, relentless fury it did reach in later years.

But in those few tragic weeks in the middle of 1940 the deep sea tug potential was more than cut in half.

The Germans captured or sunk tugs belonging to Holland and France, and those they captured they armed and used on coastal convoys as additional rescue-escort ships.

Ironically enough, some of them were attacked and were damaged or sunk by our coastal forces.

The gap had to be filled somehow.

Guarded talk about months of drawing and months of building was brushed aside.

"Here is a sound design. From that we can elaborate and in a few months we can have tugs. . . ."

A naval architect was given an outline of requirements.

A question was posed.

"Now, how long?"

The architect cogitated. "A week."

"I want those plans by tomorrow."

Lights burned through the night until pale dawn usurped them and the plans were ready.

Then to Henry Robbs, of Leith, a shipbuilding firm with a reputation for building a stout and true ship.

"Look at these plans. How long will it take you to build me a tug like that?"

There she lay, on paper, a tug of more than 1,000 tons, Diesel engined, twin screw, fitted for towing and salvage with a cruising range of more than 15,000 miles.

Cautious Scottish eyes scrutinized the plans, pondered over material available, problems of man-hour production, looked out over the wide, bleak Firth of Forth and after due consideration an opinion was given.

"Say nine to twelve months."

"I want her in three months."

The Scottish eyes blinked.

Finally: "Aye, we can do it if we get the backing."

"You'll get it."

The first big, modern rescue tug was on her way to the measured mile—almost. Truly "the oft-laid schemes of mice and men" in war time as in peace.

But officialdom had not finished. There were delays, infuriating delays, frustrating delays and prolonged discussions over comparatively minor points of equipment-points which could have been discussed and settled as the first tug was taking shape. The delays spread over months—ultimately to more than a year.

In the meantime convoys were sailing with only one tug—and that perhaps having to change over to another convoy in mid-ocean. Merchant ships were fitted with improvised towing-gear; trawlers were allocated to rescue/towage work and strove hard to do a job for which they were not fitted.

Meanwhile the perfect rescue tug remained but lines drawn on paper.

Finally the first one was built, rather more than a year after she was first drawn.

Ironically enough, the first of the class was named *Bustler*, an oblique compliment to the men who had bustled across the Atlantic in search of tugs, who had found some and had them sent over to Great Britain, but who had not stopped at that although it was called success.

A compliment to the men who had driven a naval architect until shadows lay deeply round his eyes, who had slightly shocked a ship-building firm. To the men who had got the tugs —almost.

Sad to relate, the little prototype, although little more than half the size of *Turmoil*, was sunk about this time by enemy action, but not before she had covered herself with glory and had shown the value of rescue tugs.

Instead of the three months as the experts visualized it was nearly eighteen before *Bustler* was ready for sea, and possibly a cynic might detect in the forward trend of building a slightly satirical saga in the succeeding names in the class.

Bustler was launched in December, 1941. *Growler* followed and *Samsonia* slightly afterwards in September, 1942. *Mediator* came next in June, 1944. *Turmoil* in July, 1944, *Reward* in October, 1944 and *Warden* in 1945.

Read those names in relation to the story of their conception and the irony becomes more apparent.

A 'bone in her teeth'. *Turmoil* on speed trials

Zwarte Zee, latest ship to bear a name rich in towing history

Towing thimble and shackle. When that parts . . .

Easing the tow to save fraying

Through the hurry and Bustle of effort until frustration starts Growling, then more Samsonian efforts, the subleties of Mediation through the Turmoil of effort, then Reward with Warden watching for future reference.

A neat and pleasing picture with just a *soupçon* of bittersweet about it.

Possibly there was something in the over-all planning which was not known at the time, and defies understanding today, but in certain circles the visual image of a rescue tug fell into two divisions. Some of the tugs were to be equipped with powerful pumps and accommodation and equipment for divers—in short, everything a rescue tug, or salvage tug if one prefers the term, would be likely to require in its work.

Others were to be equipped merely to tow with accommodation provided for about ninety men picked up from sunken ships. There were to be scrambling nets to be dropped over the ship's side—but no other equipment.

So be it, and so it was.

Throughout the war, particularly in the later years, the work done by tugs in all theatres would fill a book much larger than this if they were related only in bare outline.

It was singularly lacking in any dash or glamour, and on a larger canvas resembled the sections of the other forces which recovered damaged tanks, or salvaged crippled aircraft, so that they could be made whole to fight again.

Their orders invariably started: "You will sail 0400" [what impish humorist in nearly all commands had that unearthly hour at his, or her, fingertips?] "and will take in tow . . ." No flaming funnels as engineers whipped the last ounce of speed for the final blow, no depth charges poised on triggerlight catches for the last and fatal run-in, not even the satisfaction of knowing that a large and dangerous minefield was being methodically and noisily reduced to impotence. Just ". . . and will take in tow".

Or, situated at the rear of a convoy they would one night hear ominous thuds ahead, would see eerie white flares soaring

C

into the sky, would see the flash of gunfire, perhaps. Then, looming out of the darkness would come a crippled ship, her hull riven, her stunned crew bewildered. Then the rescue tug required no orders.

With almost motherly care she would edge close to the cripple, her very presence radiating comfort, a boil of water under her stern, the sharp slap of a line carrying a rocket. Soon would come the terse information from her broad after-towing deck to the bridge: "Tow all fast". Once again the cripple would gather a small white bone in her teeth and would move.

A harassed and over-pressed "Tail End Charlie" of an escort would spare precious moments for a quick look, give a sigh of relief and would hurry on to join the macabre dance of death ahead, confident that the sorely hurt ship was in good hands.

As often as not, as the convoy steamed away ahead, the thuds becoming fainter and the star-shells and flares becoming reddened by distance, sharp eyes on the tug would pick up a small group of red lights. They were little electric battery-equipped lights on seamen's lifejackets, and were visible for quite a distance on a dark night, well beyond the range of puny human voice.

Again the information would be terse.

"There's a few men in the drink fine on the port bow."

A jangle of the telegraph; sometimes the tow would be momentarily slipped, at others the whole would be manœuvred without detaching, the stout meshed scramble nets would drop over the side, strong arms would lean over, or men would even climb down the net to help the shocked men. Almost before they realized it, they were down below in a broad, multi-bunked mess deck, were holding scalding hot drinks to chattering teeth in hands which refused to stop trembling. Those with injuries were given such treatment as was available—and that often bordered on the miraculous. Once more the engine-room telegraph would jangle and the powerful engines would begin again.

That was duplicated time and time again. Finally a harbour mouth yawned. Smaller sisters would fuss out tenderly to take over the crippled ship, a hospital boat and drifter would embark the seamen. The rescue tug, in a laconic signal, would report ready for duty again.

In a fanciful moment one likes to think that the tugs which lay rusted and riven, lying in that Valhalla which waits for all ships that go down to the sea, rests content, hearing the beat of the rescue tug propellers, accepting it as a lasting requiem.

CHAPTER THREE

A SLIM, spare man with two badges in his black beret stood on the heath at Luneberg watching the humble representatives of a humiliated and beaten nation inscribe their signatures at the bottom of a document.

The tumult was beginning to die away.

A few short weeks later a mushroom of smoke climbed into the sky over an unknown and insignificant Japanese town, signifying that a mighty and powerful nation, slow to anger, had risen in its wrath, had hardened its heart and had declared its intentions clearly on the board.

To the Land of the Rising Sun it had declared: "You wanted total war. We have the means to wage it. And we will. Or let there be peace."

And there was peace.

In the passing of time men who had girded on the metaphorical sword laid their hands once more on the equally metaphorical plough. Planes which had thundered through the air to spread death and devastation themselves knew the finality of the blow-torch of the scrap yard.

Ships which had steamed the oceans, their engines seldom quiet and their guns seldom cold, lay uneasily, a dozen to a buoy, in quiet creeks, wrapped in rust-defying cocoons, mummified.

And the rescue and salvage tugs?

For them the fight was still on. So long as men take ships to sea there will always be a fight.

Some may visualize the sea as cruelty personified, others may go in terror of it, yet again others will fall under its spell as a man will fall under the spell of an exacting and capricious mistress.

Whatever the accepted view may be, one fact is unassailable.

The sea is both tolerant, to a point, and impatient of mistakes.

It is as if she is constantly reiterating: "I don't want your man-made ships defiling my undying beauty, but if you must, then the effort must be of your best. Nothing else will serve. If you build a ship there must be no error or I will find it out, and will punish. Of the men who serve, there must be no error or I will find it out, and will punish."

And punish she does, heavily.

Thousands of ships of every conceivable kind move over the wide waves, manned by hundreds of thousands of men, and it is beyond human endeavour and expectation to demand that there will never be one of those errors.

The error might arise from the dogmatic demand of a shipbuilder in the first conception of a ship; an infinitesimal miscalculation by a tired draughtsman over a drawing-board; a harassed mate will delegate to another the supervision of a portion of cargo; somebody will omit to trim a ventilator until one day a wisp of smoke reveals the extent of the error; a bone-weary seaman at the wheel, lacking supervision for a vital moment from an equally weary officer, will let the ship's head sag away in a screaming gale, and she is caught beam ends on.

Whatever the cause, the chain of events follows a defined course. Almost frantic radio signals rip through the ether. And a rescue tug sails.

She may be on station at the Azores, Gibraltar, Vigo, Brest, Cobh, in Southern Ireland, Falmouth, or up in the icy northern fiords of Iceland.

In between times she has been doing mundane commercial towing; possibly a ship has to be towed from one port to another which offers better and cheaper repair facilities. Or a ship, tired after many years of buffeting, no longer worth extensive and expensive repairs, has been towed to a breaker's yard. Or, yet again, it might even be one of the warships which had steamed on guard and watch over the very convoys attended by the rescue tug in the days of war.

But when the tow is finished, the bread and butter of daily toil earned, she returns to station, keeping twenty-four-hour watch on three or more wavelengths, the distress and the commercial channels.

That is the fight which still exists for the salvage and rescue tug. The fight to which they were committed when the tumult and shouting of war had subsided and the captains and the kings had departed.

In common with other branches of shipping, salvage and rescue tugs had suffered their losses from bombing, mining and torpedoes. There were losses which had to be made good if the constant fight against the sea was to be maintained, and if an adequate service was to be offered to the maritime world.

There were such tugs and some of them belonged to the Admiralty, which can of course find the daily round and common task for such ships. The Admiralty, viewed from a certain perspective, is merely a giant shipping company—the Grey Funnel Line—but it had tugs to spare.

So *Turmoil* and a few others dipped their white ensigns, unshipped guns, hoisted the red ensign of the commercial world and went to peace with the same aplomb with which they had gone to war.

Soon merchant ships, no longer compelled to sail in orderly and strictly timed convoys, sailed the seas on their lawful occasions and sometimes would see *Bustler*, or *Dexterous*, or *Turmoil*, or *Englishman*, or *Zwarte Zee*, or one of the others, stolidly punching into a head sea, seeming scarcely to move, and behind them would be a disabled tanker, or a super-annuated warship, rusted and unmanned, or a huge, unwieldy portion of a floating dock destined to replace the ravages of war in some far corner of the world.

Who can deny that the masters and officers of the merchant ships would spare them a kindly look and even kindlier thought as they remembered the days when those tugs were at the stern of a convoy?

The powerful Holt blue funnel boats, continuing to write

maritime history in the Far East, would see them threading a thin line towards Singapore, towing steadily at four knots. The sleek Union Castle liners streaking from the Cape would pass them abeam of Accra, outward bound for Cape Town, with perhaps another two weeks of stolid towing facing them.

Ships from the Hudson and the St. Lawrence would overtake them in the Atlantic, ponder for a moment as they recalled the latest depressing weather forecast, and would then remember that these tugs and the men who man them had done all this before.

To Istanbul, from the River Plate, from Montreal, from Singapore, and in reverse, they could be met doing the job for which they were built—towing.

An anecdote is not out of place here. A deep-sea tug left the shores of Newfoundland on an autumn tow with long weeks of breaking weather facing her; in short, the Atlantic in its autumn and fractious mood, a mood not yet attuned to its winter mercilessness.

A suave liner slipped past the tug and her tow, doing nearly as many miles in a day as the tug and tow would do in a week.

A favoured passenger, engaging the attention of a sea-wise officer, expressed surprise that a tug was so far from land in obviously boisterous weather, the tug then being three to four hundred miles on her way.

The officer replied that the liner would do probably three trips before the tug would make a landfall off the toe of south-west Ireland.

The passenger looked back at the tug, dwarfed by the size of her tow and even more so by the immensity of the liner, and frank disbelief showed in his eyes.

"But that means sailing right across the Atlantic?"

"Yes."

"That little thing?"

A more emphatic "Yes".

The frank disbelief refused to abdicate.

"But that's only a tug?"

The officer was a busy man with his lawful occasions awaiting him.

"Dine at my table to-night and remind me to tell you about just such a tug as that. It was during the war and happened around about where we will be at midday to-morrow. In far worse weather than this."

The passenger dined, and listened enthralled to a story which altered his views on tugs, at least on deep-sea tugs.

In common with the rest of the Royal Navy which expanded to enormous proportions, rescue and salvage tugs had to be manned with men who a few years before could never have visualized themselves in such a role.

The flexibility of the Briton under emergency is an old story. The bank clerk lays aside his rolled-up umbrella and becomes a deadly fighter pilot with a growing score of kills. The baker's boy drops his basket, and after a period of bewilderment and adaptation develops into a tank commander who writes a small piece of flaming history. The journalist leaves behind the smell of printer's ink and the feel of damp proofs and becomes the chilled-steel captain of a small fighting ship with the White Ensign crackling on its stern—to his own intense surprise.

And so to rescue and salvage tugs went men who had to learn as they went along—learn from mistakes until they became expert.

Over a period of time there emerged a small, compact and select breed of men who found that rescue tug work gave them what they wanted—provided the amalgam necessary to complete the formula which to them had been a story of uncertainty, of mixed emotions.

They were wanted in peace-time, there was room for them, but certain snags had to be overcome first.

A few tug owners' pertinacity finally gained the day. They visualized a need for rescue tug masters after the war and put the point to the powers that be.

"Introduce a restricted form of tug masters' ticket so that these men who have been trained and who have learned most of the tricks will not have to sit through laborious examinations on subjects which will be of no use to them. Make it an examination for Rescue Tug masters."

Finally it was done, but not before some of the men who had sailed in them had departed to other fields.

But eventually there it was. Erstwhile White Ensign tugs chartered to private firms, commanded by men who had learned the difficult art of towing and salvage the hard way.

That, to some degree, solved the problem of command. But still left the problem of crewing.

Rescue tugs—at least British rescue tugs—have no central pool of tug crews upon which to draw for their complement. They have to take their crews, and their deck watch-keeping officers, from the Merchant Service pool. In a good many cases the men who sign on tugs are men who for some reason or other—perhaps a simple one like having stayed ashore for a long time and taken a shore job—have lost their place in the pool. They can sign on a tug and having worked the necessary period, and obtained the required discharge, can then return to the Merchant Service pool.

Tug owners, and even more so tug masters, point this out as a liability. A man learns the tricks of tug work, then leaves for the Merchant Service pool because there is no scope for him.

They claim that rescue and salvage work is really highly specialized and crews should be trained from deck boy upwards for tugs, on tugs.

This is by no means outrageous. There is a parallel in the trawlers.

A boy goes to sea on a trawler as a decky-learner—and that is no idle term. He learns. His next step is to decky, or deck-hand, and after a time, possibly as bos'n, he can sit for his Fishing Mate, or Second Hand's ticket. Following more time as Second Hand he can sit for his Fishing Skipper's ticket and the whole of his sea time has been served in the highly technical work of trawling.

An A.B. from a merchant ship would not be allowed to ship as A.B. or deckhand on a trawler, and rightly so. Neither would a fishing trawler A.B. or Mate or Skipper be allowed to sign on a merchant ship or a liner as A.B., Mate or Master.

The Board of Trade has gone part way in instituting a towing Master's certificate by which a man may command a deep-sea tug and take her to any part of the world. At a tangent there is a similar state of affairs by which a man can sit for his Yacht Master's ticket and can command yachts and take them to any part of the world as a competent Master.

It requires little more than the stroke of a pen—plus a little flexible imagination—to extend this system to tug crews.

Nobody can deny the right of Captain Daniel Parker, of *Turmoil*, to be able to express the views of an expert.

While he makes no complaint about the quality of the seamen he gets aboard *Turmoil*—to the contrary, he claims that he has a superb crowd—he does make the strong point that ambition is fettered if a youngster likes tug work and wishes to go on in it.

If a young man signs aboard a tug as a deck boy, or ordinary seaman, and after a passage of time as A.B., he cannot go on to become an officer unless he puts in time as a merchant seaman and sits for a Merchant Service Second Mate's ticket. To do that he has to pass an examination which is of little value to him should he return to tugs, and in any case involves him in lengthy study.

Captain Parker's scheme, and it is advocated by many other tug Masters, is this.

Make towage and salvage as much a specialized job as trawling.

Let the tugs recruit their crews when they are young. There are boys enough still with the spirit of adventure—and if you doubt this ask the tug Masters how many youngsters ask to ship as assistant stewards, galley boys or deck boys—anything so long as they go to sea.

Once these boys are recruited and their ideas turned towards tug work let there be a similar system as that which prevails for trawlers.

From deck boy they can proceed through ordinary seaman to tug A.B. on to tug Bos'n and thence sit an examination on tug work, i.e., salvage and towage. Include a little diving work if necessary.

Having proceeded so far, a young man can see within his range of vision a job as a Mate of a tug and the possibility of being Master without having moved beyond the orbit of tug work.

Somebody may ask: "Well, who is to decide when a young man is fit enough to progress from Ordinary Seaman to A.B., and from Bos'n to Second Mate?"

From the practical towing deck point of view, and that involves seamanship of a high order, no one could be better than the tug Master himself. Having recruited a boy and watched his progress over a period of time he should be empowered to submit him for reclassification to a higher grade.

The youngster, of course, would have to sit his examination for navigation in the normal way but would not be bothered by the technical side of cargo stowage and other facts over which Merchant Service potential officers have to crouch and study at great length.

There is on board *Turmoil* a young man who could serve as a model, or yardstick if you like, for such a system.

I was walking about her deck one morning as she was on station. There had been an early morning alarm and excursion as a violent gale had hit the south-west coast of Ireland.

The excitement had died down and *Turmoil* had reverted to normal working conditions.

And I heard a voice which was completely incongruous. It was giving orders to seamen in deep lazy tones, a drawling voice which would have been quite fitting, not too early in the morning, around Mayfair.

I made myself known to the man giving orders.

He is Michael Bassett-Powell, *Turmoil's* bos'n—her foreman, if you like. He translates into action the wishes of her officers.

In appearance he could double for Errol Flynn and probably would be far more capable of winning a small war on his own if small wars *can* be won by individuals.

Topping his six feet plus he has a tanned face, a wonderful black beard and a pair of flashing eyes. Put a pair of heavy gold earrings on him and he would pass for one of the pirates which he claims were numbered among his forbears.

Before the war he was to be seen in the West End, elegant, begloved and carrying a tightly rolled umbrella, a minor executive in a West End advertising agency.

The outbreak of war found him with an N.C.O.'s rank in the London Irish Rifles—"The London Foreign Legion", as he describes it with a chuckle.

From there he moved to Intelligence and the end of the war found him restless, unable to visualize himself once more dwelling near the fleshpots of advertising and Mayfair.

To one with sea in his blood his form of escape was not far to seek—but seeking, finding and grasping were complicated.

He was offered a job as a steward on a liner and dwelt long and seriously on it as it offered him a wider horizon—a chance to escape.

He turned that down in favour of a job as a deck hand on a small tug in the Thames. "Starting in to learn what a rope was, old boy, and going on from there."

From the river tug he went, with some experience behind him, to a larger tug, the *Rumania*, a rescue and salvage tug which holds station at Dover, figuratively speaking only yards from the deadly Goodwin Sands. He had chosen a splendid place to learn the sterner facts of sea life as related to rescue and salvage.

Then "Mike", as he is known in a number of places from

Curaçao to Cobh taking in the eastern American seaboard, joined *Turmoil*, a wise, experienced tugman and still
learning.

Now he is her bos'n and is studying for his Second Mate's
ticket.

But he has had to study hard at things which, as a tugman,
will be more or less redundant to him. He will have to put in
certain time on merchant ships—with the possibility that he
will be lost to rescue tug work.

At the moment he is a tugman body and soul—but
who knows what pull will be exerted if he puts in time on
larger, perhaps more regular and more comfortable merchant
ships?

Unfortunately rescue tugs figure in no ambitious M.P.'s
constituency and have nobody to fight their cause, but somewhere, somehow, there must be somebody who can advance
their claim for a system of examination for their own work as
have the trawlermen.

By that means, and by that means alone, will this country
ultimately come to possess a rescue tug service admitting of
no peers because the men in it have grown up in it, have been
promoted in it until they reached command. The acid test,
of course, would be: should a young man pass his navigation
examination, or his qualification from tug O.S. to A.B., would
the Master of the tug submitting him accept him back in his
crew at that higher qualification?

And no tug Master in his right senses would submit a
youngster for elevation unless he was certain he was good
enough, and would welcome him back when he was elevated.

Surely it is not beyond the powers of the Board of Trade to
institute for tugs, as they have for trawlers, a specialized form
of training and qualification?

By that means we would be assured of a steady stream of
expert towage and salvage men coming into the trade.

The Dutch Government, rather more objective than ours
at the moment, has just such a system whereby tug officers are

required to obtain a special licence which can be obtained only in deep-sea tugs, and promotion remains in the tugs.

And the Dutch Mercantile Marine deep-sea towage and salvage is considered to be the cream of the sea-going profession.

Rightly so.

CHAPTER FOUR

Turmoil we have seen in brief, her measurements, her tonnage and her power, but to see her at her best is to see her at sea.

Her bridge, set well forward, is squat, wide and looks back over her almost spacious towing deck. At the fore end of this towing deck is an enormous towing winch with a central drum round which runs the heavy towing wire. At each end of the winch is a barrel five feet in diameter.

That winch is an exquisite piece of machinery despite its size. *Turmoil* can, and does, tow on that winch, which is sensitive to an increase of pull, and when that threatens to become excessive the winch automatically releases a little tow line, and when the pull decreases automatically recovers it.

She has, also, a towing hook half as thick as a man's body.

The tow line passes out to the tow not from the stern of the tug but from a point roughly amidships.

The reason for that, without becoming too technical, is that the central point gives the tug a greater degree of flexibility, which is one reason why ordinary ships, such as merchant ships or trawlers, cannot exercise the same amount of control over a tow as can a tug.

And tows, whether they be commercial tow or salvage, are not by any means the docile creatures one would imagine.

Inevitably they sheer about, charging from one side to the other so that at one time a tow might be out broad on the tug's stern by as much as 45 degrees, or more—in some instances; in heavy sea they will be even up abeam of the tug.

Then the ship will suddenly decide to sheer over to the other quarter after having pulled on the tow until it is bar-tight and twanging with an ominous deep-throated note.

From being bar-tight, as the towed vessel charges in and across the stern of the tug, the tow sags deeply until the ship

47

is wide out on the other quarter and once again the tow line vibrates ominously.

It is not difficult to imagine the constant strain imposed on the towing gear by this ceaseless charging from one side to another when it is remembered that the tow line might be anything up to 2,000 feet or more in length. The value of the flexibility of the large winch then becomes obvious.

Try taking a large and ungainly dog for a walk in the park on a long lead, with that dog deciding to investigate a number of points of interest anywhere within a wide half circle of you, and you will have a thumbnail picture of how a tug copes with a tow.

Well, there is your tug, her black hull and buff upper works and funnel giving her a distinctive air.

Now of the man who commands.

Captain Daniel Parker arrived in tugs as an afterthought. Much of his life has been spent in luxury yachts as captain, apart from a few youthful excursions into more adventurous maritime circles.

He has deep-sea fished off Galopagas and, although he is rather reticent on this point, in a more relaxed moment he seems to have a fund of inside stories of the fun and games which took place off America's celebrated Rum Row in the riotous days of Prohibition.

He is old enough to have served in the First World War, some of his service over the same waters in which he has recently made salvage history.

His first command? When he was thirteen years old.

He comes of seafaring stock and his father took him to sea on a small sailing trawler when he was not yet twelve years old.

And when the weary trawling men slept after shooting and heaving the trawl and shooting and heaving again, they left at the tiller the small and frightened boy.

Imagine him, scarcely knee high to a ship's bollard, sitting in the cold and draughty stern of the tossing and pitching

Two thousand feet astern is the *Casualty*

Casualty abeam. "Stand-by to pass tow"

Two of Smit's Dutch tugs with floating dock in tow

Turmoil with 100 feet high grain elevator in tow

fishing smack, knowing, possibly, that one error on his part could mean disaster.

Probably then, although he did not realize it, he first came to an understanding with the sea. "I won't underrate you, I won't make a lot of mistakes of the same kind, but I am so young and my ship is so small. Have pity!"

And in succeeding trips he learned. Fifty years on he admits he is still learning and still has that understanding with the sea.

". . . my ship is so small. Have pity!"

Then came the day when he had his first command. A major from a military establishment, in a burst of enthusiasm, bought himself a seven-ton yacht. Not one of the streamlined, suave yachts of to-day but a straight-stemmed, deep-keeled cutter with a fidded topmast.

(A fidded topmast is a mast in two parts, similar to some of the flagstaffs seen at yacht clubs and naval establishments to-day.)

That cutter set a clumsy jackyarder sail and in really bad weather they would have to bring her topmast down and stow it.

The soldier could steer only if she was running before the wind, and that, in nearly all circumstances, was easy.

When it became a beat against the wind, or a question of reefing, then the work fell on 13-years-old Dan Parker.

He was technically paid hand; in effect, the only sailor aboard and was in command.

From that he progressed to larger yachts, with a short excursion into the first war in armed trawlers and at the Gallipoli landings, before uneasy peace found him back among yachts.

After years of luxurious command in yachts of two or three thousand tons, with crews of 60 or 70 men, war once again caught up with him.

He helped to commission a yacht for the Admiralty in 1939, and was indeed her First Lieutenant for a time.

D

Men who could handle small ships were then at a premium because the Germans were momentarily, but effectively, winning the minelaying versus minesweeping battle.

If it is of interest (and it should be), at the outbreak of the 1939-45 war Great Britain had in service 76 minesweepers of which 40 were converted trawlers, but by the end of the war we had 1,464 minesweepers commanded mainly by Reserve Officers—R.N.R. and R.N.V.R. To meet that expansion men from all walks of life came into the Royal Navy before that battle was won, and to win it cost us 327 minesweepers and more than 4,000 men.

Parker was one of the men who came into that vast expansion and swept mines with a converted trawler fitted to fight magnetic and acoustic mines.

"There was an awful lot of monotony, an awful lot of bangs, but it was worth it. Each bang meant a mine wasted— and a ship saved from destruction," he said ruminatively.

He little knew that later in his life saving ships would be his whole concern.

When the war ended Parker, with few illusions about the sea, tried to translate his dreams of peace into a haven ashore. Most seamen have those dreams involving either a field or two and a cottage, a pub or a small shop. Parker's dreams turned towards a little shop with shelves of cigarettes and tobacco, and newspapers on the counter, and children coming in for sweets—and not too far away the sea to which he could walk occasionally and renew old acquaintance.

Of such things are dreams made of, and how quickly they dissolve under the scorching heat of reality.

Finally Daniel Parker reluctantly turned his thoughts once more towards the sea which had claimed most of his life.

Until then his knowledge of tugs had been confined largely to the fussy little craft which had helped berth the palatial yachts he had commanded—little boats at the end of a big rope.

Then he met an old friend, a captain who commanded a

deep-sea tug and was looking for a chief officer. Parker admitted cautiously that he was looking round. They talked and the outcome was that soon Parker walked up the gangway of a rescue tug as the chief officer. The tug was *Turmoil*. The two had met, the ship and the man, whose names were to be blazoned round the world.

But at that time Parker looked upon it merely as an expedient—something to fill a gap. Maybe in the near future taxation would be relaxed and big yachts would again sail— with large crews, with guests of the millionaire owners aboard —into sunny climates where the gales were few, where the sea ceased from troubling and the wind was at rest.

Turmoil's station and work was a far cry from that.

In between tows she sought the areas where the wind was vicious, where the gales were deadly and merciless.

But Fate was tip-tapping at him with its hammer, measuring him before dealing the final blow which was to turn him into a doyen of rescue tug masters, and would weld him to rescue tugs until he goes down to the sea for the last time.

And when it was ready it dealt its blow.

His captain went ashore sick and Parker was placed in temporary command. In almost hours he went out to his first rescue job, a freighter, the *Robert L. Harrison*. It was not an epic. *Turmoil* did her job of rescue neatly, without fuss—and Parker was blooded.

Her captain returned and Overseas Towage and Salvage, astute enough to recognize that they had a man of sterling value, gave Parker command of a smaller tug, the *Dexterous*, a tough little ship smaller than *Turmoil*—but a command.

The tip-tapping went on. *Turmoil's* captain finally went ashore for good and Parker moved back to her.

The ship and the man were finally together.

This was no expediency. This was a fusing together of two major forces, two supreme qualities. And between them Parker and *Turmoil* were to become household words over most of the world. To-day they are synonymous. Between

them they have fought the gales around Fastnet, the English
Channel, Irish Sea, the North Channel and the Clyde.

The *Robert L. Harrison*, the *Bisco 4*, the *Flying Enterprise*, *the*
broken, shattered half of the tanker *World Concord*. Those
rescues have been blazoned abroad so that everybody knows
at least the broad outlines.

What is this fabulous rescue tug captain like to look at,
to talk to, in action?

To be in character he should be about six feet two, broad
with it, with a voice which could tilt against a gale and be
heard a thousand feet away.

In fact he is completely opposite. He is broad, but about
5 feet 7 inches tall.

Tap at Captain Parker's door in his berth under the bridge
and a soft voice, almost inaudible, says: "Come in." Facing
you, seated on a settee, hands resting on knees, completely
relaxed, is a man with a wealth of snow-white hair. Beneath
that, black bushy eyebrows almost hide his eyes and it is not
for some time that one realizes that hazel, green-tinged eyes
have been giving one a steady scrutiny, a scrutiny of assessment.

After the snow-white hair it is the voice which leaves a
lasting impression. There is a slight, almost indistinguishable,
Hampshire burr. His slightly high-pitched voice in conversation remains on the higher plane. He seldom drops his voice
at the end of a sentence and when he does it has a curious ring
of decision.

He had been up since before four o'clock in the morning
of the day I met him standing by as a gale was blowing and
ships might be in trouble, but no weariness shadowed those
deep-set eyes.

For a while he fenced with questions of the rescue jobs he
has done, dismissed some of them with a few short, clipped
sentences until a technical point arose.

That involved consulting a chart and a towing report and
the frigidity thawed. As broad fingers once more traced a

course over the stained and figured chart the picture grew, amplified by a pencil sketch or two.

One of the directors of the company which owns *Turmoil* says of Captain Parker: "When there is a problem you can almost see Parker thinking around it."

It is an apt description. As he talks, and once again the problem of getting a line aboard a stricken ship becomes alive and vital, his eyes take on a far-away look. He is no longer talking to a small audience. He is going over the task once more, probing, pondering, trying to assess any mistakes so that they will not occur again—ever.

Occasionally, to amplify or explain a point, he refers back to his towing report, the log all tug Masters keep.

For sheer brevity concealing a wealth of action they are masterpieces.

". . . o615. Wind SSE, force 8/9. Sea rough. Tow parted.

". . . o830. Re-connected tow."

Only by constant questioning can he be spurred into elaboration of those terse entries, into a reluctant story of battling in more than a full gale once more to get a ship in tow and more or less under control.

All captains of ships, whether they be fishing smacks, trading coasters, river tugs, liners, cruisers or deep-sea tugs, are called "The Old Man" by the rest of the crew and it matters not if they are popular, feared, respected or held in contempt. "The Old Man" it is.

If there is a variation of that, then upon that variation can be assessed the affection or otherwise held by the crew for the captain.

The term "Old Man" is, of course, never used in his presence, neither is any variation.

When seamen want to reveal their regard for their captain they coin a phrase. "The Old Man" can become, in their conversation, "The Old Feller", "The Old Boy", or even "The Old 'Un", and that might be even if he were a mere stripling of a captain in his early thirties. "The Old Man" over many generations of usage has become impersonal, meaning nothing. It is from the variation that one can assess a crew's valuation.

To the crew of *Turmoil* (and it seems to be handed on from one crew to another as changes occur) Captain Parker is affectionately known as "Father".

An example? Here is one. "He's got his funny ways, has Father, but you see him getting alongside a ship in trouble, just his head above the bridge rail, white hair blowing about, and he dabs her down just off the ship's weather bow as neat as you like. No messing about with 'Father'."

Warm approval from stern critics hard to impress and please.

Like other deep-sea tugs, *Turmoil's* articles are for six months according to the Board of Trade scale and her crew changes frequently, seamen being the restless creatures they are.

But with successive crews there seems to be a degree of constant expectancy not met with in merchant ships. The atmosphere is more like a naval ship at second degree of readiness for action stations.

Men are going about their daily round and ordinary tasks with one ear for ever close to the radio room.

In that room is the latest equipment in radio, and there is maintained a constant watch 24 hours around on three wavelengths, often four.

When a call for assistance is picked up (and by some extraordinary occult means there is invariably a steward near the radio room when one comes in) all other work is dropped, the crew wait to see Captain Parker climb the short ladder to the bridge and in a few minutes, night or day, she swings away from the quay and heads for the open sea. If by any chance any members of the crew are ashore and on strict orders not to go beyond sound of her siren—five short blasts will bring them back, swearing probably, but nevertheless possessed of a feeling of exhilaration at the possibility of action.

In action—for rescue work is *all* action—Parker never hurries. His officers and his crew—and again I advance them as stern critics—say he never hurries. He approaches a "casualty" —for as such he classifies a ship in trouble—with the calm, detached air of a surgeon about to start an operation. He knows what the broad operation requires, from experience, but he watches for the minor snag, the unconsidered trifle which might build up into a major problem.

Sometimes he will circle a ship two or three times studying her before deciding to pass a tow. When he has finally made up his mind *Turmoil* is edged close in on the weather bow of the ship and away goes the tow.

That tow is worth a mention. Parker, thinking around problems, has evolved a type of tow on which most of the hard work is done on *Turmoil*.

All a ship has to do is to accept a light endless line from *Turmoil*, pass it around her bitts, or bollards, and let the tug do the rest. By a progressive series of heavier lines the ultimate and heavy tow is hauled aboard complete with eye or loop, ready to pass over the bollards.

Sometimes, if it be night time, Parker will circle the "casualty", assess her condition, estimate the position and the proximity of any danger coast, then will pass a reassuring message and will wait for daylight with risk minimized, *Turmoil* meanwhile sitting close to the other ship with lights burning.

When risks have to be taken he will take them, as he did with the *World Concord*, but in the main he prefers the cold, dispassionate approach, the calm assessment of all possibilities —then the final move in.

The simile to a surgeon performing a major operation is not so far removed. Each knows that a slip at a critical time can wipe out all the careful preliminary work and can turn the operation into disaster.

But when the moment comes for the supreme move there is no hesitation.

I wonder what some of the millionaires who employed Captain Daniel Parker to command their palatial yachts would think if they could see him at sea after many hours of travail on a rescue operation.

Whereas they had always seen the spruce, sartorially correct, brass-bound captain with not a stitch or a hair out of place they would now see a man with perhaps two days' of stubble growth, dressed in a duffle coat, and the shadows of vast weariness darkening his eyes.

They would have to admit, as they had recognized when he commanded their yachts, "There is an adequate seaman."

There can be no other sort in deep-sea towing and rescue.

CHAPTER FIVE

THE origin of deep-sea towing is no further back than the beginning of last century and is closely allied to the development of the marine steam engine.

From it grew, or evolved, the more exacting and more exciting deep-sea salvage and rescue work, both the work of Dutchmen.

For countless generations that nation of resolute people, the Dutch, have been facing up four-square to the sea in all its moods and have been saying: "Do your worst; we will meet it."

From the sea they have wrested thousands of acres of rich land to add to their small country and in doing so have learned to respect the power of the sea, its infinite capacity for ruthless and immeasurable damage—and have learned of its limitations even when allied to its companion, the wind.

They had learned, in the centuries when wind was the only means of propulsion, all that was to be learned about gaining a few precious yards against a foul wind by kedging—carrying out anchors and laboriously hauling on them—and carrying them out again. They had learned, too, of the limitations imposed on a boatload of oarsmen, no matter how powerful.

When the steam engine became related to the small ship they saw, perhaps but dimly at first, a means of defeating the frustrating delays caused by head winds, and saw a means of defeating the swift tides which flowed through and round the shallow sandbanks which cluster along the Dutch coast.

Small paddle tugs, their broad blades frantically beating the water into a froth, began to appear at the mouth of the Scheldt—and the days of backbreaking kedging and towing by oared boats were numbered.

From that point to a period when the tugs steamed over

from the entrance to the Scheldt to the Downs, off Deal and
Dover, was but a momentary transition.

In the Downs, swinging uneasily at their anchors, were
tall, many-sparred ships which had sailed two thirds round the
world, only to meet frustration when they were almost home,

One can imagine a fretting captain of one such sailing ship
striding up and down his poop, tapping his barometer,
watching the drift of the clouds, cursing the wind which seemed
to be set from the east for ever.

Then, to the east of the Downs, a broad black plume of
smoke threading off to a tenuous trail would capture his
attention. At closer range the smoke would be seen coming
from two tall funnels of a paddle tug, broad, ungainly, but
moving steadily and pushing a large bow wave in front of her,
and flying from her staff were the Dutch colours.

The captain had vaguely heard of such things in conversation in steamy bars in Penang, had even heard revolutionary
talk—by younger men, be it said—that the time would come
when all ships would make such smoke and would not need
sails, nor sailors as he knew them.

Over a large Bols gin such theories had been laughed to
scorn; those stinking smoke boxes were useful enough in the
Scheldt—saved many hours of hard pulling and helped to
berth a ship. But in the deeper waters?

Such nonsense! But here was a paddle tug coming into
the Downs, threading its way through the many ships anchored
and waiting for a fair wind.

Finally the paddles thrashed into reverse and with mixed
feelings the captain watched her approach his ship, then hand
up a long envelope to one of his mates.

In less than no time, following the orders from his owners,
the paddle tug was made fast to his bow and he was moving
through the maze of ships at three knots, bound for the
Scheldt—with the wind dead in his eye from the north-east and
not a stitch of canvas set.

He wondered, as he passed a British ship also bound for

the Scheldt, how this towing business would affect a mild
wager he had laid with the captain of the Britisher. First home
was to receive a case of excellent Bols and a dinner in the best
restaurant in Amsterdam.

As he looked back along the broad, straight wake astern of
him, and at the cluster of ships still wind bound in the Downs,
a smile played around his lips. There would be an argument,
but whoever paid for the dinner and the Bols, there would be
a topic big enough to last out the dinner—and the subsequent
proceedings.

One can imagine the conversation later in the shipowner's
solidly furnished office.

"Mynheer, that dirty smoking tug has saved me—saved
us—days, perhaps a week, because this easterly wind looks set
from that quarter. I wish she could have met me down-
Channel." The captain would climb heavily to his feet and
would spread a broad hand over the chart on the wall.

"I made a good leg from Fastnet, but once I was abeam of
St. Catherine's, in the Isle of Wight, it was tack, tack all the
time. First Barfleur, then St. Catherine's, then Barfleur again,
not ten miles gained in a day—and after Dungeness it was
torture."

Mynheer shipowner had fastened on one sentence.

"I wish he had met me down-Channel."

"If to the Downs, then why not to the Isle of Wight?" he
pondered and he scribbled a reminder to discuss it with the
young, enthusiastic owners of the tugs.

"And why not the Isle of Wight?" they reasoned, too.
"Of course it would cost more, but offset towage against the
time saved, total that time saved over a couple or three years
and it comes to nearly an extra voyage. Furthermore, with a
westerly wind set in for a time there could be towage outwards,
say to Dungeness, where the broader channel opens up."

So Channel towage was born, created by a nation of men
who had not for one moment admitted that the sea, with all
its might, was supreme.

And one morning the people of the small village of Yarmouth, just inside the western end of the Isle of Wight, stepped out of their doors to see anchored offshore a broad paddle tug, two tall thin funnels throwing up a wisp of smoke while from her staff flew the Dutch colours.

They heard the clank of her windlass as her anchor was raised and the smoke increased in density; the water was thrashed into a white froth each side of her as she bored her way out to sea, out towards a column of sea-bleached sails towering over a barque making the Needles on a starboard tack, the one of many against that damned easterly wind.

As soon as the barque's captain sighted the tug he had issued orders to his mates.

The seamen could scarcely believe their ears.

"Ha-a-a-nds to shorten sail."

With the wind from that quarter, with that icy bite in it they had expected many more weary watches, many more calls of "Ha-a-a-nds to lee braces", had expected many more wearying tacks with but few miles gained.

And here it was "Shorten sail."

From the ship to the tug a stout tow would be passed and the ship's seamen would make the most of the opportunity for a brief chat with the men on the tug, the men wearing the faded, much-patched blue trousers over their wooden clogs.

As the tow would be made fast they would ask: "Where are you taking us?"

"Rotterdam."

"Rotterdam! Why, that's still hundreds of miles away. We'll . . ."

"You'll be there in two days, not more than three, if the weather holds."

Two or three days instead of perhaps fifteen. Unbelievable!

So to lie idle on the fo'csle head while the smoke-belching tug heaved away, making a creaming bow wave under her own bow and that of the sailing ship.

Beachy Head, then Dungeness, South Foreland, the tossing Goodwin lights, then the Scheldt in a matter of days.

The picture begins to take a definite form.

If down to the Solent, then why not to Falmouth, where so many sailing ships called in for their first orders after a round the world trip? To tow ships of other nationalities who have to reach the prosperous South Wales ports, or the Mersey.

So sea towage was born, from the start—nay, from the conception—a lusty, powerful creation.

From it (a latent twin, if you like) came salvage.

Ships which had sailed the world went ashore in thick weather, gear which had been hammered in the long passage revealed weaknesses in the demands of many tacks.

Here, again, it was no longer a question of laboriously laying out kedge anchors, driving weary man-power to produce an extra ounce from already straining muscles.

Tows were carried out to the tugs, whose paddles churned madly until the stricken ship, creaking and groaning, would be hauled off the rocks. Or, dismasted and helpless, she would be nursed into harbour to lick her wounds and to be repaired.

The last century drew to its closing years with deep-sea towage an established industry, with international competition giving it an added stimulant—but with the Dutchmen still supreme in that sphere.

In yet another direction—with generations of experience behind them—the Dutchmen were also supreme. Reclamation work from the sea was being undertaken in the far corners of the world, shipyards were being built up, dredgering and floating docks and a host of other schemes requiring vast engineering projects were beginning to turn what had been trackless jungle or sun-bleached beach into commercial enterprises.

The gigantic plants for these projects were erected, numbered, taken to pieces again and shipped out to South America, Central American and Asian destinations.

But the dredgers, floating docks, large pumps and even more complicated engineering erections, while they worked efficiently in Holland failed to work at all or did so only indifferently when re-erected abroad.

Possibly it was unskilled native labour, or the lack of proper supervision engendered by a mixture of gin and the debilitating effect of the tropics—but the fact remained that efficient and complicated masses of floating machinery ceased to be efficient and became more complicated under a hotter sun than that which shone on the land where they were made.

It was a challenge to the Dutch engineers and it was accepted.

They would tow the plant, vast and unwieldy as it was, across the world so that all that was required when it arrived was to start it working.

Men lacking both the courage and the vision to undertake such a task, but not lacking a critical tongue, prophesied that the bed of the oceans, from Rotterdam to Sao Paulo and to Penang, would be littered with expensive machinery—assuming that the tows could reach the open seas, which they doubted.

The problem of bunkering the coal-burning tugs was resolutely tackled; bunkering stations were set up, some of the tugs sailed almost rail down to the water with extra bunkers stowed on deck and the dredgers, floating docks and other plant set out. And arrived.

Once again give imagination a little rein and conjure up the looks on the faces of masters and crews of tall and graceful sailing ships as they snored along at eight or nine knots under a blue, cloudless sky and suddenly sighted first a cloud of black smoke then, closing it, saw two tugs, white water boiling under their sterns and behind them, wallowing drunkenly, the towering bulk of a dredger complete, such a dredger as they were not expecting to see until they were into the mouth of their own river Scheldt.

Possibly the man at the wheel, holding the tall ship to her

course with maybe a turn of the wheel, allowed his hands to drop in surprise until a roared curse—and the rap of a spoke against his head—brought him back to a regard for the fitness of things.

The steam tug, now beyond its infancy, had laid the foundations of what were to become the three broad pillars of ocean towage, ships, dredging plants and floating dry-docks.

They had overcome the frustration of the adverse wind in close waters, they had overcome the partial failure of plant when re-erected abroad and their squat, powerful hulls had become as familiar in the waters of the sampan and junk as they were among the shallow outriggers of the West Indies and the mud-laden waters of the North Sea.

They were operating in the seas of the monsoons, the typhoons, the hurricanes, instead of in the fury of the eastern Atlantic and the Channel.

Those lashing winds would take their toll of shipping in just the same way as the winter gales they were used to. Ships would run into trouble, would be driven ashore, would be dismasted. Under any climate that was something the men of the Dutch tugs could understand, could assess in the full—and could thereupon render aid.

Soon ship masters of every nationality carried on their bulkheads the rough positions of Dutch tugs so that in an emergency they could be called upon.

Shipping agents, too, had such information to hand and many a strong, stout ship continued to sail the seas because a tug flying the horizontal red white and blue ensign had been able to render assistance when it was most urgently needed. Tugs journeyed over two thirds of the world to deliver a vast and ungainly piece of machinery—and stayed there a year or more finding towage and salvage work.

Deep-sea salvage and towage had grown up from lusty babes to a young but virile force in the years that Queen Victoria reigned.

From a tentative essay just beyond the Scheldt estuary to a

world-wide passage in about sixty years because somebody had thought of putting a steam engine in a small ship.

In the period of the middle century the limitations of the paddle tugs were beginning to be recognized. They were shallow, as befitted ships which had to work in the few fathoms off the North Sea banks. They were powerful—there is nothing more powerful afloat even to-day than a paddle steamer, which can work up to full speed in a few hundred feet—and by the same token, with her paddles thrashing in reverse can stop herself in almost her own length.

For deep-sea work, however, their lack of draught is a liability.

The stern screw, or propeller, began to come into its own and ship designers—especially when drawing the lines of a tug—found they could place the screw deeper and still deeper so that it was continually biting into the water no matter how much the tug would pitch.

By a process of evolution—the result of thinking men observing and passing on their observations—it was found that the best place to which a tow could be made fast was near the centre of the ship so that at almost any angle up to ninety degrees the tug could still apply its enormous power. Towing hooks moved further forward from the stern—which had seemed a logical place up to then—and the towing decks became broader and longer. To make this so the bridge had to be moved towards the bow until finally the tug as we know it to-day was evolved.

Look at the pictures of *Zwarte Zee* or *Turmoil* to see what I mean. They have powerful, bluff bows which rise upwards full enough to ride over almost any sea. Then comes the bridge and behind it a short boat-deck.

From that, at a point almost half way along the length of the tug, starts the towing deck; low, squat, with a wealth of room in which the crew can work.

After a fairly wide experience of ships ranging from large merchant ships, destroyers and minesweepers it was a revelation to me to see a tug of a thousand tons buckle down to a tow. The engines started, took up the strain, the tow became momentarily tight, then sagged as the compensating winch paid out. The low, powerful after-deck seemed to sit down hard on the water to get a good grip. Once the tow was balanced and moving, the broad beam, carried almost to the end of the tug, began to take effect. The bluff bow parted the seas; they roared past cresting and instead of them tumbling aboard over the low after-deck, as I had expected, they slid past innocuously, the towing deck lifting easily over them because the point of contact, the towing winch, was amidships, not pinning her stern down as a tow would to an ordinary ship not designed for it.

As the early aero designers groped courageously into the unknown in building the crude planes of fifty years ago, so the Dutch tug designers experimented. Sometimes they failed but more often they succeeded, passing on their knowledge until we have the almost perfect towing machine in the ocean-going tugs, built to stand up to any weather, built to tow in any weather and manned by men who have evolved with the tugs.

E

CHAPTER SIX

To SPEAK of Dutch tugs is to speak in almost the same breath of the firm of L. Smit and Co., Internationale Sliepdienst, Rotterdam-International Tug Service, of Westplein, Rotterdam.

This firm has grown up with the industry—as industry it is.

To-day it has a vast fleet of tugs. It has 19 ocean-going tugs equipped with every modern towing rescue and salvage appliance. In addition, they have more than 20 harbour tugs, small, powerful little instruments which work in the waterways of Rotterdam for berthing and unberthing shipping.

The names of some of their deep-sea tugs reflect the passionate regard the Dutchmen have for the sea.

There is the *Zwarte Zee*, the *Gele Zee*, the *Oceaan*, the *Oostzee*, the *Roode Zee*, the *Noordzee*, the *Poolzee*, the *Witte Zee*, then there is their river-class tugs named after rivers. They have the *Thames*, the *Humber*, the *Tyne*, the *Maas*, the *Hudson* and the *Schelde* and the *Ebro*.

With the exception of the *Schelde* and the *Ebro* they are all motor tugs, modern, designed and built to tackle anything towable. I am quite convinced that if some engineering genius succeeded in putting the Blackpool Tower, or the Eiffel Tower, on a floating pontoon and asked the firm of Smit if they could tow it to Sydney the short answer would be "Ja" and to it would be added an approximate date of arrival. And it would arrive.

Smit and Company's records of tows over the past sixty years are a true reflection of the growth of ocean towage and the names of tugs engaged in those early tows are part of that history.

Mere figures make dull reading in themselves but ally them to something attempted something done and they can take on an unusual magic appearance.

In the past sixty years Smit's have towed nearly a hundred floating-docks to all parts of the world, voyages covering a total of nearly 300,000 miles, and have lost only two.

The names of some of the tugs engaged in those early, almost exploratory, voyages are names which are revered in deep-sea towage and have been handed on.

For instance, the bare records show that two Dutch tugs, the *Oceaan* and the *Oostzee*, set out from Rotterdam with a floating dock weighing 1,350 tons for San Paul de Loanda, a distance of more than 5,000 miles in 1896. And arrived safely.

Again, down the list a little the tugs *Zwarte Zee* and *Oceaan* towed a 17,000 tons floating dock from the Tyne to Bermuda.

The list goes on and as ships became larger and demanded more room in the floating docks so the tows became heavier.

The *Roode Zee* and the *Zwarte Zee* took in tow a dock of 25,000 tons from Barrow in Furness for Rio de Janeiro.

They were tugs with but a fraction of the power of the modern towing leviathans, but sturdy tugs, brave tugs with equally sturdy and brave men manning them, men doing a job only dimly realizing, perhaps, that they were making history.

The list expands; the old "Smokey Jans", coal-fired smoke-belching tugs gave way to the modern, sleek motor tug, but the names remain, passed on almost with reverence.

Towards the end of the long list there appears the names the *Zwarte Zee*, the *Thames* and the *Witte Zee* taking in tow in 1939 a floating dock weighing 31,000 tons from Portsmouth to Alexandria.

The war clouds loomed darkly and from 1939 to 1946 there are no entries of ocean tows at all. Some of Smit's tugs were caught up in the German war machine—and were sunk.

Others, further afield on the day the German bombers leapt on Rotterdam, escaped and did valuable rescue work in convoy. They, too, suffered the bombs and torpedoes of outrageous war and when peace finally came there were long gaps in Smit's list of tug names.

The gaps were a challenge to this company, as much a challenge as the frustrating easterly winds had been to the earlier seamen.

And in the passage of time the gaps were filled; again the *Zwarte Zee* and the *Oceaan* and the *Witte Zee* and the other legendary names appeared once more, this time on modern, sleek motor tugs, some of them with as many thousand horse-power concealed in their engines as their predecessors had hundreds.

Yet, powerful as they are, sleek as they are, the last word in design as they are, they can do no more than did the old "Smokey Jans" of the past half century.

Once again I will let cold figures produce their own magic, their own stories of tows which even to-day must appear phenomenal.

Smit's towing record, beginning in 1892 (and that was not the actual beginning of their concern) up to the beginning of 1953—sixty years—shows that their tugs have towed 907 ships, 627 obsolete hulks, 2,469 dredgers, 3,992 lighters, 279 cranes, 84 floating dry-docks, 518 other craft, a sum total of 8,874 tows. Cold figures? Read them in relation to the places to which recent tows were made.

Mainly from North Sea ports, where the building yards lie, to South America, to Fortaleze, to Bahia, to Rio de Janeiro, to Porto Alegre. To African ports, Dakar, Conakry, Abidjan, Lagos, Cape Town, Beira. To Indian ports and up the Persian Gulf. To Suez, Choramshar, Karachi, Calcutta, Colombo, Bangkok, round the Malayan maze, to Djakarta, up to Osaka in Japan, to Hong Kong, south to Albany, Sydney and Melbourne in Australia.

Across the Western Ocean to New York, to New Orleans, through the Panama and to Colon, south to Callao, up to Portland and Seattle.

The world bestrode a dozen times by those three pillars of ocean towage, floating docks, ships and dredgers.

And in what period? The tows I have itemized and the

places represent only two years' work in the records of Smit's, during the years 1951-1952. Imagine what the records would have to show if lines were drawn on a world map for every tow they had done in the past sixty-odd years.

From the moment a tug takes over her tow until she finally delivers it she faces the multitude of hazards the sea can produce for those who go down to it in ships and feel the fury of its wrath.

Even ships designed and built to withstand the raging of the seas find trouble and weariness, are broken and engulfed.

Imagine the problems facing a tugmaster with a colossal unwieldy tow astern of him, a tow which is a mass of right angles, inanimate, sluggish, at times stubborn, a thing to be nursed through gales.

There were losses, inevitably, but when the figures are ranged alongside the number of tows over the half-century they appear to be incredibly small.

From 8,874 tows of varying descriptions between the years 1892 and 1952 Smit's tugs lost only 60, most of them in the embryo years of deep-sea towage, 50-odd between 1892 and the late 20's and the few others since 1946.

And now to the tugs which bear the illustrious names which are part of deep-sea towing.

The tugs which bore the names originally have gone the way of all ships, others which followed on in the passing years have also moved out of the picture, some to honourable retirement in shallow waters, others to sail under another flag and not taking with them the names. The names have remained to become as much an integral part of Dutch maritime history as that nation's continuous and greater fight against the encroaching sea.

The queen of the fleet of deep-sea tugs is the *Zwarte Zee*, a powerful motor tug of 836 tons in her 197 feet of length. Her 4,000 horse-power engines can drive her at 17 knots and she has a cruising range of 20,000 miles.

Like most of Smit's tugs, she is completely equipped with

every form of salvage gear and fire-fighting appliances, and carries divers among her crew.

Next to her in size is the *Thames*, 602 tons in her 172 feet of length. They both draw more than 16 feet—*Zwarte Zee* in fact draws a maximum of 19 feet—giving them a considerable and constant bite into the water no matter how they pitch.

A far cry from the old paddle tug drawing 4 feet or so with thrashing paddles on each side.

Their counterparts in British tugs would be the *Turmoil*, larger than *Zwarte Zee*, and *Dexterous*, about the same as the *Thames*.

Next are the *Oostzee*, *Roode Zee* and *Oceaan*—fabulous names over the past sixty years. They are smaller, of 500 tons and 147 feet long with 2,000 horse-power engines. Small if compared to *Bustler*, *Turmoil* or their sister ship, the *Zwarte Zee*, but powerful nevertheless.

In 1952 the little *Roode Zee*—I use the term "little" relatively, —towed one of the world's largest suction dredgers, *La Cruses*, from Cristobal, in the Panama Bight round the coast to Porto Alegre half way down the east coast of South America. Truly is the word "little" merely relative.

The even small river-class tugs, the *Loire*, *Humber* and *Tyne* are but 386 tons and are 131 feet long, but that pint-sized giant *Tyne* towed two barges and a dredger from Rotterdam to Callao, Peru, a voyage of 7,200 miles. Anything more resembling a nightmare at sea than a dredger I have yet to visualize. Imagine its creaking, unwieldy bulk rolling and pitching, sometimes astern, sometimes sheering out to one quarter then the other, sometimes hanging back sullenly snatching at the tow, at other moments without warning gathering impetus down a steeply sloping sea and charging in full fury at the little tug which constantly maintains the mastery.

No wonder the Dutch tug men have become a breed on their own, a type evolved and developed as the Cape Horn sailing ships produced their breed of iron men in wooden vessels.

The record goes on almost endlessly. Tow after tow devouring almost astronomical distances, fighting weather and sea—and arriving with almost monotonous regularity.

One tow which intrigued me was that of the *Zwarte Zee*. She took over three war-battered Canadian naval corvettes—a thousand tons each—in Vancouver and towed the three of them down the west coast of America, through the Panama Canal and across the Atlantic and to Kiel in 1951. That was a voyage of nearly 10,000 miles.

A photograph taken of the *Zwarte Zee* and the three corvettes at the beginning of the voyage shows that *Zwarte Zee* is as long as those trim little fighting vessels and in fact looks sturdier, due perhaps to larger bridge and short, squat funnel.

Yet from such ships, lively and tossed about as they were, and small escort ships (it was said with a degree of bitterness and weariness that they could pitch and roll on wet grass) we used to watch rescue tugs at the stern of a convoy and wonder how men could live on them; they were taking such a hammering.

Zwarte Zee made light of her tow; she took the three corvettes on towing hawsers of varying lengths, brought them over an ocean where they, too, had helped to make tragic history, and arrived within hours of her estimated time of arrival.

Smit's tugs, of course, are available for salvage as are other tugs under other national flags. In the past few years they have maintained station at places like the Hook of Holland, Flushing; Dournez, in France; Cobh, County Cork; St. John's, Newfoundland; Coruna, Spain; Horta, Azores; St. George, Bermuda; Nassau, Bahamas; and Colombo, Ceylon.

That same map which shows the activities of their tows in the years 1951-52 also shows some formidable rescue operations. They did two rescue jobs off the south-west coast of Ireland, one in the Bay of Biscay, two in mid-Atlantic, towing one to the

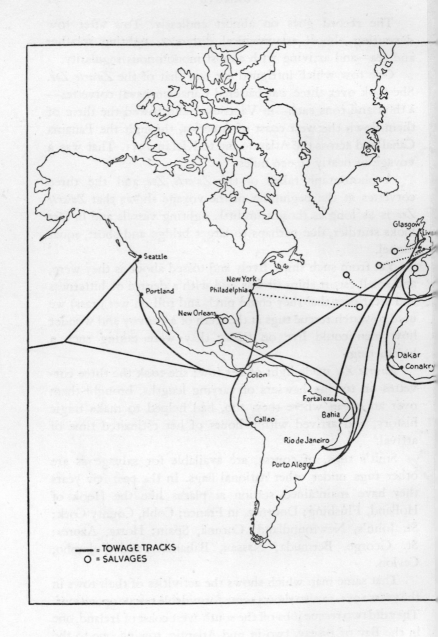

Seattle

Portland

New York
Philadelphia

New Orleans

Colon

Callao

Fortaleze

Bahia

Rio de Janeiro

Porto Alegre

Glasgow

Dakar
Conakry

= TOWAGE TRACKS
O = SALVAGES

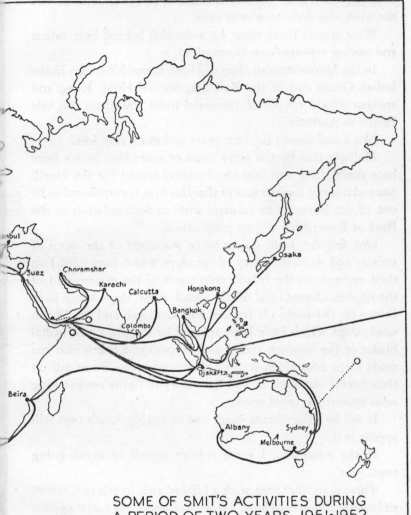

SOME OF SMIT'S ACTIVITIES DURING
A PERIOD OF TWO YEARS 1951-1952

Azores and the other two-thirds of the way across the ocean to Philadelphia. There was another taken to New Orleans, and the work was done in winter time.

What stories there must be concealed behind bare rescue and towing reports from those tugs!

In the Mediterranean they did four rescue jobs, two in the Indian Ocean end of the Red Sea, one off Hong Kong and another over a couple of thousand miles tow from the vast Pacific to Australia.

Not a bad record for two years and not a ship lost.

Multiply that by the sixty years or more that Smit's have been functioning and add their coastal record for the North Sea and it is not hard to accept that this firm is considered to be one of the foremost in salvage with an accumulation in the Bank of Experience of vast proportions.

One fine day I am going to be possessed of the devil of activity and write the story of the ships which have ended up their voyages on the treacherous sands of the eastern end of the English Channel and off the Dutch coast, ships which have driven on the rocks off Ireland and Cornwall and the Welsh coast, ships which have been speared by the black and brutal blades of the Scottish coast, and of salvage work which has made them float again so that they could once more sail on their lawful occasion. It will be a story of fights against long odds against the cruel coast.

It will be a fascinating story and inevitably Smit's tugs will appear in it.

In the meantime, I must confine myself to ocean-going tugs.

There is another firm with a history rich in salvage, rescue and towage, but where Smit's story starts with the battle against shallow waters, adverse winds and the shifting sands of the North Sea this company's background is written against a ruthless, savage rock-bound, merciless coast, the Bay of Biscay.

It is the Cie. de Remorgue et de Sauvetage of France.

All of that company's tugs are named "Abeille" with a following number.

They, too, are manned by men who were born with the sound of the sea in their ears, who had their first lesson of the unending ruthlessness of it drummed into them almost as soon as they could toddle. Bretons, men with a thousand years of salt intermixed with the blood in their veins.

The "Abeilles", too, can be found, when they are not engaged in towing, where the sea can be at its worst—and it can be no worse than on their own doorstep, that menacing curve from Ushant to Finisterre, Biscay Bay.

Deep-sea tugs like to be mildly secretive. They like to think that between tows they are securely hidden away from competitors in harbours from Gibraltar to Lerwick.

It is a mild deception because they know, and shipping companies know, that they are to be found, as policemen are to be found, in or near the areas where there is likely to be trouble.

All the major tug companies have contacts right round the coast, men more or less connected with shipping, men who will let them know at any time, day or night, when a ship is in trouble in that area, whether she be driven ashore or labouring heavily and under difficulties. And it requires no great stretch of imagination to realize that the contacts will report whether tug X, normally on that station between tows, is there or not.

Study the map which embraces the north-west coast of France, the western toe of England and the south-west coast of Ireland.

That area is a considerable portion of the famed Western Approaches.

Ships can sail the whole world round but to reach the major ports of Europe they have, ultimately, to come into those gateways. It was a point which had not escaped those responsible for submarine warfare in the two great wars.

In peace time those gateways also offer their hazards.

That area is the birthplace of some of the worst weather in

the winter months to be found anywhere in the world. The gales build themselves up to a fury further out west and by the time they reach the area they are possessed of their full fury. The sea floor shelves about there and the seas build up into steep, vicious mountains of water.

Any time from October to March can be a tough time thereabouts. That is why the deep-sea tugs of the major countries have bases there for their craft so that they cover it in between tows.

Even now, as I write, there would be possibly half a dozen tugs or more not further away than a day's steam from any point in that area. Any ship in trouble and sore distressed could be almost certain of getting aid in a short time.

For the sake of the record, pursue the point a little and take in the whole of the entire Atlantic eastern seaboard. There are tugs based at Azores, Gibraltar, Lisbon, Vigo, Corunna, Brest, Ushant, over the area I have mentioned, in the Clyde, Stornoway, Scapa, Lerwick, and Iceland.

A comprehensive coverage by any standard, and it would have to be a set of circumstances bordering on the fantastic to arrange that a ship *could* be in trouble in those south-western approaches and not be able to obtain aid in the space of a day.

Yet it happened.

In the closing hours of the year 1951 a gale of ferocious intensity hit the eastern waters around south-west Ireland, the Bay of Biscay and the English Channel.

The air was filled with radio messages from ships which, labouring heavily, were out of control, had lost propellers, ships which wanted help.

One such ship was the American freighter *Flying Enterprise*, commanded by Captain Kurt Carlsen.

A wind which reached hurricane force overcame her; she sent out a distress call and help was available.

Smit's tug *Oceaan* was ordered to go to her aid. But as *Oceaan* hammered into the gale she received a call from *Zwarte Zee* that she, too, was in difficulties with a tow in the north end of the Bay of Biscay. The rugged, rock-bound coast of France loomed in *Zwarte Zee's* lee. Help was imperative.

So far as *Oceaan* knew then, the *Flying Enterprise* had been abandoned by her crew, was drifting beam ends on, whereas *Zwarte Zee* was in extreme difficulties with lives at peril on both tug and tow.

Oceaan rightly turned away; lives come first.

And *Flying Enterprise* was left to battle it out alone for several days with the lone Carlsen on board.

Turmoil was in the area but she, too, was committed.

She had passed *Flying Enterprise*—without seeing her—as she had slammed from Cobh to a point west of the Fastnet to assist a tanker, the Anglo-Saxon ship, the *Mactra*, which had lost her screw in the same hurricane.

Other tugs in the area were heavily committed either with tows or were standing by stricken ships.

It was a set of circumstances which in all probability will not arise again in another hundred years.

So on to the story of the *Flying Enterprise*—and of the rescue tug *Turmoil*.

CHAPTER SEVEN

IT HAD been a turbulent Christmas for the captain, crew and passengers of the American freighter *Flying Enterprise* on that Christmas of 1951.

A savage wind had rolled and tossed her about on Christmas Day but those of the ship's company who had been able to had made as much as they could of the festive season.

Now, on December 26th, the merciless Atlantic, lashed into a rage, awaited them. Winds rose to hurricane force—60-65 miles an hour—as the *Flying Enterprise* was level with the south-west coast of Ireland, as bad a breeding ground of evil weather as Cape Horn itself.

At St. Anne's Head, on the toe of Wales, a few miles to the eastward, gusts of 95 miles an hour were registered.

Captain Kurt Carlsen, captain of the *Flying Enterprise*, descendant of a long line of Danish seamen, with as much salt water in his veins as there is blood, decided to heave-to until the weather eased up slightly.

For two days the ship lay hove-to, barely making headway against the steep, short seas, which, coming over the shallow shelf a few hundred miles westward, changed their characteristics from the long and towering waves, with more than half a mile between them, to the quicker tempo of three cresting seas in that distance, each of which would hit the ship with devastating power.

Through the wild Boxing Day and the next day the ship was nursed with consummate care, captain, officers and ship on the one side and the ever-ravenous sea on the other, each waiting for the other to show a sign of weakening.

A mightier sea than the others reared its head somewhere out in the western ocean, gathered two or three smaller seas into its bulk and roared along on destruction bent.

78

Flying Enterprise, groaning and creaking, met its full fury. Down went her head into it; she shuddered and reeled and when the sea had passed on *Flying Enterprise* had changed from a battling ship to a crippled hulk.

A split had developed in her deck and she lay over on her beam ends.

A frightening picture to daunt the stoutest of hearts.

Her staccato distress signal went out and ships fighting the same hurricane turned from their course.

All the ingredients were there of a shipping disaster so frequently acted out in the stormy Atlantic that it seldom rates more than a few paragraphs in the newspapers. But it was the beginning of an epic which captured the imagination of the world to such an extent that up-to-the-minute details of the fight were given on American radios and it swept other events from the front pages of newspapers.

Because the world loves a fighter.

The first ships to reach the *Flying Enterprise* were the U.S. transport *General Greely* and the U.S.S. *Southland*. It looked as if it was going to be a task all too familiar and all too frequently enacted in the north Atlantic.

It was assumed that the *General Greely* and the *Southland* would take off the passengers and crew of the *Flying Enterprise* and would wait until the doomed ship plunged from sight.

By superb seamanship the *General Greely* and *Southland* did get close to the *Flying Enterprise* and 35 members of the crew and her few passengers, including women and children, were rescued.

Captain Kurt Carlsen, Master of the *Flying Enterprise*, declined to leave his ship while she still floated. To landsmen that may seem a futile gesture, but to seamen it is quite understandable. While she floated she was still his ship, his to command, his to nurse, if possible, through a crisis, leaving him to decide when all hope was gone.

And to leave her then—not before.

The *General Greely* stood by for three days while the gale

tore at the *Flying Enterprise* which lay over at an alarming list. Then the weather moderated slightly.

In the meantime other ships were closing in.

The United States Navy had dispatched the destroyer *John W. Weeks* from Plymouth to the scene and in the meantime also diverted the U.S. transport *Golden Eagle* to relieve the *General Greely*.

Commander W. L. Thompson, captain of the destroyer *John W. Weeks*, slammed her into a western gale from Plymouth to the *Flying Enterprise* at a speed which slightly shocked some of his officers and crew but which earned the respect of seasoned seamen.

From then onwards, until relieved by another destroyer, Commander Thompson hovered near the listing ship, transmitting signals, closing in to pass hot food and drinks to Captain Carlsen, inching his destroyer close to until they could almost see the whites of Carlsen's eyes.

To assess the risks he took one has to realize that the *Flying Enterprise* obeyed no metronomic rules. A commanding officer of experience, called upon to close another ship in heavy weather, studies both the movement of his own ship and that of the other, and they have a regularity governed partly by the sea and partly by the captain's handling of his ship. Even then, a false move, a moment of delay, can spell death and disaster.

Imagine, therefore, the deadly dance with the destroyer and the *Flying Enterprise* as the partners. Commander Thompson was determined to get hot food and drinks, and other requirements, to the brave man who had steadfastly refused to leave his ship, and get them aboard he did.

The listing ship, lying over almost on her beam ends, would sullenly lurch up to the top of a sea, would hang poised for a few moments, then would swoop drunkenly down into a hollow between seas and would swing round broadside on before starting another climb.

But Commander Thompson's will and skill prevailed and

Towing deck awash

Flying Enterprise alone, adrift and with a heavy list. Is that Carlsen framed in the higher part of the bridge?

the hot food and drink were passed; one or two lots were lost but the remainder did get aboard to the man who was attempting the impossible.

Sufficient importance has never yet been attached to those forays of Commander Thompson's. How much comfort did Kurt Carlsen draw from those supplies? Immeasurable.

How have you felt when you have battled home through a boisterous December wind which has torn and battered at you, and then you have found a warm cup of cocoa, or a bowl of soup, waiting for you?

Multiply that a hundred times and you can then begin to assess the moral value of Commander Thompson's effort.

It was not merely risking a half million pounds' worth of ship for a gesture.

By some curious quirk the weather relented after three days and the sea became just an uneasy swell—but ominously promising more bad weather.

Flying Enterprise had been drifting south and east of the spot where she first met disaster with the faithful *John W. Weeks* in unceasing attendance.

To most people, even to experienced salvage and towage men, it was just a question of time before *Flying Enterprise* took her final dive. The destroyer would be on hand to rescue Kurt Carlsen, the world would admire—briefly—the heroism of the freighter's captain and the skill and seamanship of the commanding officer of the destroyer. And would turn to the next item of current interest.

When the weather moderated, however, those same experienced men figured that the *Flying Enterprise* had at least a sporting chance. She was drifting towards half a dozen ports capable of taking her in. From somewhere she had got a reserve of buoyancy—and a spiritual pugnacity—which kept her afloat.

Well, where were the rescue tugs which sit waiting, poised for just such an emergency?

F

The wonderfully equipped Dutch tugs were battling in the Bay of Biscay.

And where was the other character in this drama, the tug which was to become almost a household name in this country? TURMOIL.

She was towing another ship which had run into trouble in the same gale which had smote *Flying Enterprise*.

The tanker *Mactra* had sent her request for assistance on December 26th—Boxing Day. She was west of Fastnet Rock and steering trouble had developed.

Turmoil sailed forthwith and contacted her.

As she plugged into the steep seas with *Mactra* in tow *Turmoil* listened in on three wavelengths, the commercial and the two distress wavelengths, and heard some of the story of the *Flying Enterprise*. To her it was just another story of a ship in distress, not varying a great deal from the one she had astern of her.

She was not to know that a stubborn, obdurate man who was an amateur radio fan was using his hobby to talk at close range to the destroyer circling and closing his ship like a distressed mother bird.

Turmoil plodded on. And *Flying Enterprise* drifted.

The year 1951 drew to its close. The riotous crowds joined hands in Glasgow and London and a hundred cities and sang the old out and the new in.

And a few hundred miles to the west a Homeric fight was to begin; the arena was being cleared.

Flying Enterprise would just not sink and suddenly she became a commercial proposition.

The Dutch tug, which was visualized as being nearest to the *Flying Enterprise*, was suddenly involved in trouble which ruled it out. *Turmoil* had in the meantime reached Falmouth with the *Mactra* and lay with her all night.

She had gone out to do the job for which she was built; she had taken a lame ship in tow and had brought her to harbour and to safety.

What went on over the telephone in London, E.C.3, concerned her not until it was translated into orders to sail—that was something Captain Parker could understand.

So, as *Flying Enterprise* wallowed and drifted through the weather-beaten days and hights *Turmoil* completed one job and lay rolling uneasily in Falmouth Roads until daylight of January 1st. Twelve precious hours—twelve hours for which Captain Kurt Carlsen and Captain Dan Parker of *Turmoil* would later have bartered at least a fragment of their immortal souls.

On January 2nd *Turmoil* sailed from Falmouth to contact *Flying Enterprise*, which up to then had been putting up a solitary fight, with the lone, heroic, almost tragic figure of her captain scrambling about on board.

The world's knowledge of events in and around *Flying Enterprise* was, of course, hours, even days, behind.

So far as Fleet Street and its newspapers were concerned at that time, a ship's company and passengers had been rescued, a ship was lying on her beam ends and the fate of her captain was not known. It was variously stated that he had been washed overboard, that he had failed to reach the *General Greely* or the *Southland*—in short, nobody quite knew where he was.

I remember studying a picture of the ship, taken from the air, by that famous photographer Stanley Devon, and a forlorn picture it was indeed.

Wind-lashed spindrift was sweeping across her, the photograph was indistinct; remember that it was taken from a pitching aircraft in driving rain with sharp outlines blurred.

Because I was more or less accepted as an expert in naval and maritime matters Henry Clapp, the editor of the *Daily Graphic* (later to become the *Daily Sketch*) and Kerr Robertson, the then assistant editor, put the picture down on my desk and said, in effect: "Study that. There are several stories about the captain of this ship. If he is still aboard, then it is a REAL

STORY. That blurred object on the deck might be a man. Now, is it?"

Magnifying glasses were borrowed, and they merely emphasized the blur. But there was something near the winches which I could not explain. There was a conglomeration of lashed-up topping lifts, derrick downhauls, which, under the spindrift-blurred picture, could with a little imagination have been described as a human figure.

There was one portion, a half-bent outline which from my experience had no right to be there unless it was a human being leaning against the tilt of the ship.

WAS IT? Edition time was getting near and the editor and assistant editor were faced with this decision: were they to print a blown-up picture of this indistinct figure and say: "Here is the heroic captain of the *Flying Enterprise* still aboard his stricken ship," with the chance that a few hours later it would be announced that he had been drowned?

Surgeons and lawyers often want a second opinion, and sometimes journalists welcome one. Serving on the *Daily Graphic* at that time (and still on the sub-editorial staff of the *Daily Sketch*) was a colleague, Herbert Inman Field, who had been at sea for years in both the Royal Navy and the Merchant Service.

Bert and I, delving into our experience, studied the picture long and intently.

There was nothing that should have been on that spot on the after-deck of the *Flying Enterprise* if she was properly prepared for a winter north Atlantic crossing, unless it was a human being, and the only human being who could be on *Flying Enterprise* at the time the picture was taken was her captain, Kurt Carlsen.

We jointly committed our reputations—if not our immortal souls—as maritime experts and said: "There is a man."

The *Daily Graphic* published the picture and a few hours later the captain of the American destroyer, Commander Thompson, signalled that he was standing by, had made contact with Kurt Carlsen and was endeavouring to pass hot food and drinks to him if unable to persuade him to leave.

Bert Field and I had a quiet drink the next evening in mutual admiration of a joint effort.

The last word remained with Bert.

"Of course, she is an American ship, and that figure *might* have been some sea lash-up-and-stow strange to us."

It wasn't, and Carlsen was still aboard. The destroyer captain was considering getting a tow aboard, but if there is anything less suitable for towing in bad weather than a destroyer I have yet to meet it.

Flying Enterprise was drifting south and east, diagonally from the western toe of Ireland towards the rock-bound coast of northern France with a strong wind veering from south-west, through west, to north-west.

Telephone receivers were replaced with the sharp smack of finality in E.C.3—and *Turmoil*, leaving her lame tanker *Mactra* in the capable hands of harbour tugs, sailed to rendezvous with the *John W. Weeks* and *Flying Enterprise*.

For five days the American freighter had fought it out alone, until even the elements relented and gave her a smoother sea.

Captain Parker had no guesswork to do in this case. The *John W. Weeks* was almost as close to *Flying Enterprise* as a Siamese twin—where *John W. Weeks* was, there would be the freighter.

In the early hours of January 4th, Commander Thompson sent this heartening signal:

"*Turmoil* alongside *Flying Enterprise* at 11 p.m. last night. Preparations now under way for taking *Flying Enterprise* in tow."

Commander Thompson added: "The *Flying Enterprise* is still listing 60 to 65 degrees to port and is down slightly by the head. Rudder and screws are clear of the water and the rudder is winging free. Ship will be towed by the stern to prevent further flooding. Captain Carlsen is cheerful and grateful for food, cigarettes and magazines passed to him earlier."

Kurt Carlsen has always been taciturn to a point of brevity about what went on in his mind in the lonely hours he spent on *Flying Enterprise* from December 28th until the night of January 4th. It does not require a wealth of imagination to be with him.

Beneath his feet his ship lay over at an alarming angle. The slope of an average roof is about 40 to 45 degrees—try walking on that! His deck was 60 to 65 degrees, was wet, treacherous and heaved and pitched beneath him.

During the daytime he had a fragment of comfort in the proximity of the destroyer which at the bat of an eye would lift him to safety if his ship looked like foundering under him.

The long, dark, cold winter nights must have searched down into the depths of his courage—and found it not wanting.

In bad weather the best of ships groan and creak; the wind finds small holes in ventilators and around stays, the subsequent moans and whines rising and falling in a steady symphony which becomes a discord when some part of it suddenly stops.

But Carlsen had a new set of sounds to torture his dark hours.

There was the sudden rush of water which flooded part of his ship. It swept back and fro to the pitching of the *Flying Enterprise*. The trapped waters, raging to join the vaster sea outside, would crash against the watertight bulkheads in thunderous booms.

There were unexplained thuds, there were sudden high-pitched screams as tormented metal momentarily succumbed to strains far beyond that for which it had been shaped and designed.

There must have been a thousand heart-starting jolts through the nights when Carlsen said to himself: "This is it. This is where I leave you."

Imagine, therefore, the joy and jubilation in his wearied heart when he saw from his wet and cold quarters on the bridge first the red then the green side-light and the mast-head lights of the *Turmoil* as Captain Parker brought her close to *Flying Enterprise* to prepare the preliminaries for his tow.

"Here at last is a tow; here at last is something which can hitch to us and help us."

Flying Enterprise and Captain Carlsen had by now become as one.

The sea at this moment began to growl a threat. It was as if it said: "This is my victim. I have played roughly with it, I have played gently with it, I have smashed it, I have pawed it softly like a cat stirring into movement a mouse before finally dispatching it. I will have no other taking part. This is my kill."

The deceptively oil-smooth seas began to wear white caps; an errant wind occasionally whipped the tops off and flung them in stinging spray, a faint reminder of the power of the elements.

And to Captain Dan Parker, on *Turmoil*, a major problem had poised itself. He had every facility conceived by man for towing a ship of any size anywhere, under almost any conditions. There were wire ropes which take terrific strains, there were nylon tows, gracefully thin but with the wiry strength and indestructibility of a ballet dancer.

But on the *Flying Enterprise* was one lone man, wearied after five days and nights of incessant strain. Could he haul aboard the light line required to get a tow to her to get her under control?

The usual practice is for a rescue tug to close to within a hundred feet or so—little longer than a cricket pitch plus the length of run of a slow bowler—and fire a light line across the stricken ship, either by line-firing gun or by rocket. Two or three men (and they are invariably forthcoming) will struggle to get aboard a succession of thicker messenger lines until ultimately the main tow is hauled over, made fast and salvation begins.

Captain Parker pondered that problem through the night of January 4th without finding what he considered an adequate answer.

Now, when *Turmoil* closes a ship in trouble she fires a light line, little thicker than a fishing-line. Once that is aboard, and a few men can haul on it, it pulls aboard an endless line but little thicker. Both ends remain on *Turmoil*. Once the light line is round a bollard, or bitts, *Turmoil* heaves away, passing a succession of thicker lines until in the end the main two passes over to the ship.

It is as simple as a woman with an endless clothes line pulling away, pegging her clothes on, and pulling a little more line until the clothes spread out to dry, except that instead of clothes it is *Turmoil*'s main tow which passes to the ship and returns aboard round the crippled ship's bitts.

That morning of a wind- and sea-lashed January 4th, Captain Parker had to think out a way to get a messenger-line aboard *Flying Enterprise* where it could be handled by one weary man.

Turmoil took risks to get close enough to *Flying Enterprise* to pass the first line. Carlsen heaved and strained with the two ships, the rescuer and the would-be rescued swaying together and surging apart like dancers in a grotesque square dance.

Carlsen had to heave one-handed. He was standing on a sloping surface of 60 wet, slippery degrees, a moment of lost footing and he would have been into the sea with probably a broken limb at least as he crashed down across the deck.

It was beyond human endeavour, although he struggled to get the line aboard, winning a few inches and losing them again in one vicious lurch.

Aboard the *Turmoil* men watched him with knuckles squeezed white as they saw him heaving and straining, as they watched him pause for breath, head bowed, red, raw hands hanging on to the few precious feet he had gained. Then a surge of the ships would drive them apart, the line would tauten and the precious, soul-searing, hard-earned feet would be lost in seconds.

First at the stern of the *Flying Enterprise*, then at the bow, *Turmoil* wriggled in close until the ship towered over the squat tug. Lines were fired, Carlsen scrambled along the decks and the drama was played again.

Oh, just for one more man aboard, a strong man who would help to hold on to the precious few feet of slack each time it was gained!

Commander Thompson, although fully knowing that his paper-thick hull would be riven if the *Flying Enterprise* hit her, contemplated getting a small party of men aboard to help.

He asked for volunteers, making it clear that once aboard, the men would have to stay in the fight to the finish, would be on that sea-lashed, comfortless wreck until she finally reached harbour and safety, or until they had ultimately to admit defeat and take a chance of being picked up perhaps in the darkness.

When the shuffle of feet of volunteers had died down it looked as if Commander Thompson would be left alone on his ship, with *Flying Enterprise* populated by the entire crew of the *John W. Weeks*.

There is little doubt that into the darkness of the merciless Atlantic Commander Thompson smiled a grim little smile, a challenging smile as he said to himself: "See! That is what you have to fight." And a thought perhaps chased through his mind: "But for the fact that this is MY ship, MINE to command, you would all be half a jump behind me."

Five times *Turmoil* risked damage, possibly disaster, in closing *Flying Enterprise*. Five times the light line went true, five times Carlsen heaved and strained with bursting lungs and throbbing muscles. And five times the line parted, or slithered away from him.

Such men are not defeated easily. In fact they know defeat only when their eyes are closing for the last time; when they know that when they open them again they will have the answer to all things, will open them after a defeat which becomes lasting victory.

Carlsen, almost out on his feet, once got to within twenty-four inches of getting a line secured aboard. One arm was hooked round a bitts, those powerful steel, foot-thick squat columns on a ship's deck which look like over-size collar studs. One arm round the bitts, the other heaving and straining at the line. Twenty-four inches; a surge together by the two ships would have given him ample scope.

The Atlantic must have chuckled as the two ships surged apart; the slithering, slipping line tore through Carlsen's raw fingers, the twenty-four inches became twenty-four feet and again defeat.

Commander Thompson radioed: "Carlsen has decided to conserve his strength until new gear is rigged by *Turmoil*. Difficulties . . . were caused by a 70 degrees list which made Captain Carlsen hold on with one hand while handling extremely heavy gear with the other.

"Increasing heavy wind and rain squally hampered salvage, but Captain Carlsen remains cheerful and confident, saying only patience is needed."

In all, Captain Parker of *Turmoil* had made eight attempts to pass a tow, five of them coming near to success. Captain Parker and sleep had been strangers for long, long days by now.

Remember, he had gone out on December 26th to search for a crippled tanker, had found her, had towed her in, and had sailed to the assistance of *Flying Enterprise*. It was now ten days since he had snatched more than the odd half-hour doze, forty-eight hours since he had contacted *Flying Enterprise* and had tried at intervals to get lines aboard.

But there was no rest for him. As the long winter night closed in he got *Turmoil* up to *Flying Enterprise* and turned on his searchlight.

There *must* be some way of getting a tow aboard.

There was, and it happened in the twinkling of an eye. It was one of those moments when fortune, in a fragmentary gracious mood, will dangle success before one's eyes and will say: "Here it is. Take it *now*!"

And the moment was taken.

CHAPTER EIGHT

CAPTAIN PARKER once more edged *Turmoil* in close to *Flying Enterprise*, so close that with reasonable luck the line could be passed direct to Carlsen. In the remnant of a day of disheartening failure the two ships closed until the gap was only feet. First *Turmoil's* powerful stern hung poised above the stricken ship, then the *Flying Enterprise* lurched drunkenly to the top of a swell and towered threateningly over the tug twenty feet below.

Standing on the deck of the tug was a young man who, as Chief Officer of the tug, had worked unceasingly in the efforts to pass a tow to the weary man on the freighter.

He was 27-years-old Kenneth Roger Dancy, a son of Kent who had joined the *Turmoil* only a few days before she sailed.

Kenneth Dancy had no vast experience as a tug officer, but he did have wide experience of the sea. He had lived, in his imagination, with Carlsen, had heaved and strained in sympathy with the weary man on the freighter.

Kenneth Dancy, son of the postmistress of a small Kent village, Hook Green, near Tunbridge Wells, had served at sea in merchant ships from the time he was sixteen.

When he received a telegram advising him that he was to relieve the Mate of the *Turmoil* he had but a hazy idea of what his duties would involve, but comforted himself with the knowledge that so far as seamanship was concerned he could fill the bill.

He little realized that in a few days he would jump—or scramble—a few vital feet which would be blazoned round the world as "Dancy's Leap" and would pass into almost deathless legend.

Parker knew that unless Carlsen could get that tow aboard all his efforts would be as nought. So did Dancy.

The two ships closed; there was a moment when they hung together, poised at the top of a sea, with only feet between them. There was a crash as they met.

And Dancy leaped. Carlsen was no longer alone.

Seconds afterwards the two ships drew apart, with a twenty feet gap of water widening to thirty, then sixty, until *Turmoil* lay off at a distance.

Only Carlsen could tell us of his feelings when he found Dancy scrambling over the acutely sloped, sea-lashed stern. Only Carlsen could tell us of the overwhelming relief he felt at the presence of another human being.

Kenneth Dancy was nearly six feet tall, muscular, young, strong, just what was wanted to add that little extra strength to make fast the tow.

There was little time for self-congratulation. Two admirable seamen met briefly with a handshake, hanging on by their spare hands—and settled down to a night's vigil as Parker wisely decided that unless the weather got worse he would leave it until daylight to pass another tow, one which this time, he felt, would be secured.

The entire population of Hook Green had followed the published and broadcast accounts of the attempts to take the *Flying Enterprise* in tow, feeling that they had almost a proprietary right in the tug *Turmoil*.

When the news spread that Dancy had leaped to the *Flying Enterprise* the people in the little village were electrified—but not entirely surprised. They remembered the boy who would climb a tree or take a dare before he went to sea and grew up rapidly—as boys do grow into men in the twinkling of an eye when they go to sea.

The *Turmoil* and the *John W. Weeks* circled the drifting ship through the night. The predominant thought was that come daylight the tow would be passed—of that there was no doubt. But for the *Flying Enterprise* the immediate future was unpredictable. The sea was beginning to growl its anger—was beginning to reassert its claim to its victim. At any time during the night a bulkhead, tortured beyond bearing, might give way, might collapse, and the drifting ship would give one last lurch and would sink, leaving two brave men in the water.

The seas raised themselves to crested heights and through the night Captain Parker and Commander Thompson watched her narrowly. The only link was Carlsen's amateur set, working from a jury-rigged aerial, which he was using sparingly as his batteries were getting low.

The blackness had barely given way to the first pearly glint of winter dawn when *Turmoil* edged in again.

Phut! The rocket-gun rapped, the line soared truly and through red-rimmed eyes Parker watched Carlsen and Dancy heave aboard the light line. The thicker line followed. The line's weight made it sag depressingly. Dancy hunched his broad shoulders—one can almost hear him gasp: "Come up, you . . ."

"ALL FAST!"

Turmoil's radio operators had resolutely kept their traffic down to essentials—had refused all demands on their sets except those dealing with the tow. The destroyer had acted as link with the outside world, a world which by now was waiting with baited breath.

Commander Thompson's radio operators maintained unbroken contact with both the U.S. Admiral in Plymouth and U.S. Naval Headquarters in London.

And soon the world knew.

"*Turmoil* has *Flying Enterprise* in tow."

That night the B.B.C. broadcast a weather report which had an ominous interest.

". . . In areas Shannon, Biscay and Plymouth winds will be strong to gale force . . ."

A frightening prospect.

Normally a wind coming from astern, with a heavy sea accompanying it, is not such a menace as a sea coming from ahead. Because a ship is moving with it the effect is somewhat the same as a boxer riding with a punch and robbing it of much of its weight. In fact, an experienced officer has to ensure that he does not travel at the same speed as the sea, otherwise he is liable to be pooped, have the sea engulf his ship and probably swing her beam on to the next and be at the mercy of the full weight of the sea along her whole length.

There was little prospect of *Flying Enterprise* travelling at the same speed as the sea. She represented the problem tow of all problem tows.

She was down by the head, with her stern high in the air, she was over on her side, with a list varying from 55 degrees to 70 degrees, and she was partly full of water which was slashing to and fro, altering her balance. And to add the supreme problem, she had a split the extent of which could only be guessed at. At any moment, due to pressure from the sea, or by the strength of the tow, or both, the split could without warning develop into an ever-widening gap, leaving two halves of the ship to wallow and founder.

When Captain Parker's hand sought the handle of his engine-room telegraph all those problems were running through his mind. And the predominant one was: "How fast can I tow her?"

Let there be no doubt about it, *Turmoil* was powerful enough to have towed *Flying Enterprise* at three times the speed she did, had the ship been whole. Through similar weather a few days before he had towed a larger ship, upright and with only propeller trouble, at a steady five knots to safety, with a little in hand.

But *Flying Enterprise*, over on her side, was the plaything of the sea. She would hang back, dragging like a half-trained dog on a lead, snatching at the vital tow, demanding unceasing attention from the tug captain.

Then, without warning, urged on by a capricious sea, she would lurch, swing off at an acute angle, slide down the glassy slope of a towering sea at a frightening speed and, having gathered up some slack of the tow, would threaten to turn beam on to the next sea.

At times *Flying Enterprise* was nearly at right angles to the *Turmoil*, but all the time she was being coaxed and nursed nearer to safety.

Through that day Roger Dancy and Kurt Carlsen got to know each other without much conversation. They were quartered in a little steel box-room on the bridge where Carlsen had fixed for himself a sort of bed on the side of the room. He found and helped Dancy to fix up another and then they got down to the remnants of a plum cake.

That cake is worth a short anecdote. When daylight came after the first night of disaster Carlsen had scrambled about his ship searching for food. He had found a large cake which the cook had made. It had a hole through the centre—nobody knows why—and through it Carlsen thrust his arm. He wore it like a gigantic bracelet, nibbling at it when he felt the need.

Later, of course, the destroyer passed him hot food and drink, but that cake must have been wonderful.

It is worth mentioning here, too, that after Commander Thompson had taken terrifying risks two or three times to get his ship close in to the wallowing freighter, risking a submerged mast or derrick stabbing through his thin hull, Carlsen signalled: "Don't risk it any more. You are taking quite a beating. I'll wait until the weather moderates. Your ship is too valuable to risk."

But Commander Thompson persisted and finally the food and drink were passed to supplement the cake.

The weather on January 5th decided to set the stage for a little cat-and-mouse play with *Turmoil* and *Flying Enterprise*. The sea dropped, not to a degree of glassy smoothness but to an uneasy swell. The wind, too, hid its power.

And there was progress.

To understand one of the many problems facing Captain Parker on *Turmoil* it is necessary to study the map of the area.

A triangle with one point based on the south-west toe of Ireland, the second touching Falmouth and the third point resting on Brest, the north-west corner of France, gives you the stage for the drama. *Flying Enterprise* had drifted, driven by the wind and sea, along the base of the triangle towards the French coast. There would seem to be a choice of towing to the French ports or to Falmouth.

Influencing that choice were two things. It was possible that with the promised breakdown of the weather *Turmoil* would be caught off the rugged French coast with her crippled ship in tow and nowhere to go except on to disaster.

On the other hand, with the wind and sea helping, at least a little, Falmouth was the obvious choice, and if the weather did break down, then there was the whole of the western part of the English Channel in which to attempt to ride it out, even up as far as the Isle of Wight.

Carefully, juggling with his engine revolutions, Parker steadily edged *Turmoil* towards Falmouth, gaining a few miles on a north and easterly course, and each mile he progressed the odds against him shortened.

By this time a deep friend, if of short duration, had departed.

The *John W. Weeks*, dangerously low on fuel oil, had reluctantly departed for Plymouth and had been relieved by the American destroyer *Willard Keith*, commanded by Commander Leslie O'Brien, which took over the role of hovering mother-bird and acted as a source of communication between *Turmoil*, *Flying Enterprise* and the outer world which waited anxiously for every word.

There was little the two men on board the *Flying Enterprise* could do except keep an eye on the tow—no mean task as it meant a dangerous scramble to the bow of the ship. They were of course soaking wet, and Dancy has related that they tried without success to dry their clothes with candles, the only form of light they had.

On through that day and through the night *Turmoil* delicately nursed the *Flying Enterprise* and it became a race against time and against the weather.

People, with but little conception of the problems involved,

Flying Enterprise takes a sheer to port under tow. U.S. destroyer keeps
close station

No hope of passing a tow at this end

Carlsen struggles with tow passed to stern. 'Old Glory' whips from temporary staff above him

have asked: why did not another tug fasten on to *Flying Enterprise* in the next couple of days and increase the speed of tow and so bring salvation closer in shorter time?

Was it commercialism which dictated it? Was it the view: I am fast to her, she is my prize and the rest of you keep at arm's length?

A fatuous claim, but one which has been made and must be explored and refuted.

There was a powerful French tug, the *Abeilles 25*, hovering in the background, quite capable of putting a line aboard now that *Flying Enterprise* was steadied and was making progress.

And, further to refute the commercialism taunt, there was *Dexterous*, a tug belonging to the same company as *Turmoil*, sitting handy to offer any help required.

But *Flying Enterprise* was split. In fact, one of her engineers, John Edward Drake, in evidence at a later enquiry, said he saw a crack develop half an inch thick near number three hatch and described how the crew had worked with chain blocks to keep it from widening.

To the best of everyone's knowledge, it was those chain blocks which were possibly holding her together.

A 100 per cent addition of tow power might have increased her speed by two, possibly three, knots, and yet might have torn the hull in half in a matter of an hour or two.

Towing *Flying Enterprise* was not a matter of producing power and force; those were available in overwhelming numbers. It was a problem in nursing—and as too many cooks can spoil a broth, so too many nurses can kill a patient.

There were men on the bridges of the tugs, and men ashore, with a lifetime of experience behind them. Had they considered another tug essential, rest assured that a second tug would have been ordered to make fast a tow.

It makes me extremely angry when self-appointed critics and experts, with no more experience of the sea than an occasional trip to the Continent or from the mainland to the Isle of Wight, express dogmatic opinions without any knowledge

G

at all of the power of the sea, of its infinite capacity for damage, and of the skill required to bring a ship alongside a quay in a flat calm, not to mention handling a ship at slow speeds when a gale is blowing and seas swing ships together and apart again over a gap of 100 feet in a matter of seconds.

By those who have ability to assess all possibilities it has been almost unanimously agreed that all that could be done for *Flying Enterprise* was done, and was well done.

Nobody felt this more than the two men keeping their vigil on *Flying Enterprise*.

Dancy has told since of their short but eventful stay on the ship. There they were, living in that small room on the bridge, a couple of mattresses jammed against the angle of a bunk. They were virtually standing on the side of the room, the floor having become a side.

As the ship lurched the green curtains, already hanging at the grotesque angle of 60 to 70 degrees ("nice green curtains they were, too; fitted over a porthole"), swung over occasionally to the full 90 degrees, then slowly dropped back.

How many times did they watch the curtains swing out, hang poised, and how many times did they hold their breaths until the green fabric gradually swung back again? It must have been hundreds.

They didn't talk much about ships, not even about the *Flying Enterprise*. She was so close to them that there was no need for her to be a topic of conversation.

Carlsen told Dancy about his home and his family in America, and Dancy told Carlsen of Hook Green, in Kent, "Where we hardly see anyone strange," Dancy relates having said. And little did he know that millions of people knew not only of him, but of Hook Green where his mother sold stamps to the villagers—even knew that she was seeing an amateur theatrical show when the news was broken to her that he had joined Carlsen on *Flying Enterprise*.

Often they would sit in silence, even snatching a little sleep, listening to the symphony of noises, of low-pitched groans and creaks as the hull laboured, to the moan and whistle of the wind, each with his ears tuned to detect something different in the sounds, something which would give them warning.

Night succeeded day and the tow went on. In the dawn, a wild wind-whipped dawn, the two men set out along the crazily tilted deck to attend to the tow. They had been fighting against the constant enemy of towing, friction and wear.

It was as if the threatening sea had waited in ambush for them to leave the comparative security of their small room. As they scrambled along the water-lashed deck to inspect their end of the tow a sea higher and more powerful than the others which were buffeting the ship reared up and swept over her, and them.

Let Dancy describe it: "A large sea seemed to come from nowhere. Carlsen was lower than I was. He staggered, lost his grip, and was covered by the sea. Then I saw him hanging on. It seemed an eternity as the suction of the water dragged and dragged at him until I thought he could hold on no longer. When he did drag himself clear he was completely exhausted."

The possibility of injury following a sliding crash down the steeply tilted deck was always a risk they had to take. So far as was possible, either Dancy or Carlsen, or both, crawled about the ship trying to assess the extent of the crack and determine whether it had remained half an inch wide, whether it had widened or whether any new cracks had appeared.

Furthermore, they had to combat chafe in the tow. There was a lighter moment when Carlsen explained to the tug and destroyer that some excellent butter which the *John W. Weeks* had sent over had proved to be a superb element for reducing friction where the tow was fast and where it led out of the bow.

Imagine the two men, both experienced, having scrambled over the grotesquely tilted deck and having found that the working of the tow had started chafe, thereupon holding a meeting to decide how to reduce that chafe.

There was oil and grease in plenty on the ship, but it was

impossible to get at it. Would there be enough to scrape from the bearings of the winches on the main decks? There was another scramble—to meet disappointment. The sea had cleaned it all off. Hands rubbed at unshaven chins as they pondered over the problem. Grease there would have to be. Call the *Willard Keith* and ask for some? A possibility, but it would mean risking the close approach of the destroyer and that was something Carlsen did not want.

Then a smile broke across his weary and lined face.

Back they scrambled again to the cramped and cold quarters. From the scanty provisions Carlsen pulled a couple of packets of rich creamy butter. Again the bone-risking scramble, one hand for the ship and one for themselves.

The butter, rich, yellow, was plastered over the chocks which were worn silver white by the friction and chafe. The audible creak as the tow rubbed was reduced. The rich yellow rapidly turned to a dingy brown, then to black, but the butter had served its purpose and the tow moved silently, effortlessly, in a sawing motion. The friction was gone.

The radio operator's eyes arched upwards on the *Willard Keith* when he received Carlsen's terse message that they had used butter to reduce chafe on the tow where it was fast. He queried the word "butter" twice.

The commanding officer of the destroyer grinned when he heard it.

"Excellent stuff, too. Tell him he can have a large can of it if he wants it."

Turmoil and *Flying Enterprise*, by now committed to a north-easterly course towards Falmouth, made slow, pitifully slow, progress, but it was progress despite the worsening weather. The hours grew into days and nights.

The weather had, to the night of January 8th, pursued its cat and mouse tactics. It would threaten to blow, ease away to buoy up hopes, then growl again occasionally.

Then the growl grew into a sustained snarl.

Captain Parker on *Turmoil* and the commanding officer of

the destroyer *Willard Keith* watched with growing concern the way the solid seas were sweeping over *Flying Enterprise*.

They could see that it was impossible for the two men on the ship to clamber forward to inspect the towing gear, which consisted of a heavy quick-release shackle, a towing shackle and a wire bridle, besides the part of the tow which led outboard over the *Flying Enterprise's* bow.

Carlsen's radio batteries were running low, he used the set only when essential, so for nine hours, as the weather steadily worsened, there was nothing but silence from the *Flying Enterprise*.

Then in the early hours of the morning of January 9th, at 1.30 a.m. to be precise—that dreadful hour when men's vitality and courage are at their lowest ebb—there came the dread cry:

"Tow's parted!"

The savage sea had torn its victim away once more from the *Turmoil* and had so set the stage and the time and conditions that it was impossible to pass another tow immediately to the stricken ship.

Turmoil's powerful winch swiftly retrieved the forlorn, slack tow which told its own story. The sea had called in its ally, chafe.

The tow had parted close in to *Flying Enterprise*, leaving aboard the heavy gear.

From that moment saving life became the dominant factor.

On that drifting, buffeted ship were two brave men who by every measure had a right to be saved, and would be saved if human endeavour could do it.

The quartermaster's hands on the wheel of the destroyer *Willard Keith* tightened momentarily as he was given his orders; the commanding officer, trained in the difficult and fine art of keeping station on the ship ahead—and that is by no means as easy as it looks—edged his ship up until her bows were almost overshadowed by the *Flying Enterprise's* towering stern; the destroyer edging into the broken water left behind by the wallowing freighter was taking a chance a minute. She was not following a steaming ship; she was following the broken plaything of a capricious sea which was ambitious enough to visualize the warship being involved and becoming another victim.

Away a little on the weather bow of the *Flying Enterprise* was the frustrated *Turmoil*, her captain bottling down under ice-cold calm the rage he felt against his old foe, the sea.

And all this on a gale-lashed, cold winter morning with the darkness only a few degrees off being completely opaque, in a morning when the world slept.

There was one redeeming feature. Captain Parker's decision to aim for Falmouth was overwhelmingly confirmed.

Falmouth lay less than 60 miles away when the tow parted. *Flying Enterprise* had the entire northern half of the channel in which to drift without getting into more serious trouble.

Had the course been towards a north-west French port, then only that disaster a seaman fears could have awaited her That was a lee coast, a rockbound destroyer of ships.

The captain of the French tug *Abeille 25*, a powerful rescue and salvage tug which had stood by through it all, upheld that decision later when he stated to the French newspapers—and to me personally—that had he been towing *Flying Enterprise* he would have taken the same course as *Turmoil*—for Falmouth. He described in support how his own return to Brest, unencumbered by a tow, had been rough and difficult.

There spoke the voice of experience.

CHAPTER NINE

THROUGH the remainder of that dark January night *Flying Enterprise* rolled and pitched sluggishly and when pale dawn came it was obvious that any hope of passing a tow to her had shrunk to vanishing point.

To close her would have been asking for trouble. All that could be done was to keep near so that if she gave up the struggle the lives of the two men aboard could be saved.

It seemed that *Flying Enterprise*, drawing on that something which mere man does not understand, even when he builds a ship, was determined to fight on alone. Through the night and the depressing dawn she struggled alone, for more than 20 miles on a true course, the identical course that Captain Parker would have towed her. It was slower than he would have liked; she was moving at a bare knot and a half—call it two miles an hour—but she was moving towards salvation.

Through the short winter day the destroyer *Willard Keith* kept faithful close watch, and near, and ready to take the slightest advantage of any slackening up of the weather was the equally faithful *Turmoil*.

The reports from the destroyer were depressing. *Flying Enterprise* seemed to be lower in the water; she did not appear to be lifting quite so high after a heavy sea had swept over her.

In Falmouth enthusiasm had almost reached a pitch of hysteria.

Flags were prepared, people drove in from many miles around in readiness to welcome in the *Flying Enterprise* and the gallant tug *Turmoil*.

With that inexplicable avidity with which this nation will elevate a Test Match, or a celebrated divorce case, to all-absorbing interest so the country took to itself the story of the *Flying Enterprise-Turmoil* fight to beat the cruel sea.

There was no need for preamble. Men in bars and offices, and factories, and women in dwindling food queues went straight to the heart of the matter.

The newspapers kept the story as up-to-date as they could from edition to edition and even the austere B.B.C. permitted a little of the enthusiasm to creep into its almost emasculated digest of the day's news.

"She's still afloat." "*Turmoil* is waiting to put another tow on board." "Only fifty miles to go." Then with a knowledgeable glance at the weather over Glasgow, or Sheffield, or Birmingham, or Bristol—that of course giving no indication of the weather in the western Channel—people would add: "If it keeps like this they ought to make it."

There was no need for any more definite identification. One newsvendor near Charing Cross had a contents bill saying "Fifty miles to go. Still fighting."

But the day went hard. There was no chance to pass a tow and *Flying Enterprise* was getting lower in the water. She was more sluggish, she was reeling to the continual punching of the relentless sea.

Would the fight never end?

Towards midnight the weather became worse.

In a million homes people listened to the brief midnight summary of the news, heard that *Flying Enterprise* was still in the ring battling it alone with the two men still aboard, put out the cat, put out the lights and retired to their well-earned rest.

On *Turmoil* and other attendant ships, on *Willard Keith* the watch went on. In that opaque darkness a ship was battling— a ship which *Turmoil* had towed for 250 soul-searing miles before the tow parted.

Each plunge of her dark bulk beneath the sea might mean the last. There might come the moment when she would not rise again.

How valuable would have been those vital 24 hours had *Turmoil* been fast just that much earlier! But Fate had willed it otherwise.

Naval officers the world over are not given to flamboyant excursions into deathless prose. When they send a communication they send facts, and little beyond that.

So from the moment of the parting of the tow, and of the long night and day when ships waited, anxious to reconnect, let the dispatch from the destroyer *Willard Keith*, the faithful successor to the *John W. Weeks*, tell the story.

The *Willard Keith* times her signal to the United States headquarters in London 0145, Jan. 9, and being meticulously Navy it gave the state of the weather first.

Flying Enterprise had again by then been alone in the fight for 24 hours but *Willard Keith* followed age-old protocol.

Her message ran: "Midnight: position 49.27 north. 05.07 west. Sky overcast, occasional rain squalls. Sea rough, 10 feet swells, wind westerly 30 knots."

There in a few words you have the stage setting before the incidental music dies away and the actors take their places before the curtain rises on the next act.

The signal continues: "*Flying Enterprise* still has good righting movement, with only small change in list or roll. Eight p.m. radio conference, Carlsen expressed appreciation for messages from parents (which had been transmitted by the *Daily Express*) and for message from Admiral Carney (U.S. Navy)...."

"Said he was deeply touched to know that so many people in the world were interested in seeing the little *Flying Enterprise* reach port."

Having briefly sketched over the social matters, the *Willard Keith* got down to brass tacks: "Plans for re-rigging two include rigging lines round bitts at bow to give Dancy and Carlsen a firmer footing from which to work. No attempt to be made before daylight. Weather still makes any plan impossible now. Dancy and Carlsen retired about 9 p.m. after hot coffee."

The *Willard Keith*'s commanding officer completely omitted any reference to his own effort in closing the wallowing hulk until a light line could be passed and by it hot coffee and a

meal had been hauled over to *Flying Enterprise*. That risk he
dismissed as not worth a mention, as part of the job, but it had
meant creeping up to her, with debris slashing around until he
was close enough to pass the line. An error the length of an
arm's span could have spelled disaster.

The dispatch continues: "Tow line apparently broke near
bow chock of *Flying Enterprise* due to chafing (the pitiful supply
of butter having given out) leaving short length of tow,
quick-release shackle, towing shackle and bridle on board
Flying Enterprise.

"Quick-release shackle was damaged during the night and
in order to clear it Carlsen had to cut it away with a hacksaw.
Carlsen and Dancy managed to cut it loose while solid water
and spray broke over them, occasionally knocking them down.

"The task now is for *Turmoil* to pass the eye of the towing
wire with the new shackle to the *Enterprise*, after which Carlsen
and Dancy must connect this shackle to the main shackle
already on board."

To digress for a moment. These shackles mentioned are
heavy steel U-shaped shackles possibly four inches in diameter
and weigh anything up to 30 pounds or more.

Imagine those two men, those seamen of inexhaustible
courage, hanging on grimly by one hand and cutting through
that stubborn steel, more than half the time submerged in the
cold water which tore at them with tremendous power.

At least they deserved life even if the ship plunged beneath
them.

The despatch continues:

"The same wire will be used. It is a new one capable of
74 tons pull and was first used on the *Enterprise*. Prior to this
storm the *Turmoil* reported about thirty tons pull on the wire."

The amount of pull on a towing wire bears no relationship
to the weight of the tow. When a tug takes a ship in deep-sea
tow the towline sags into the water in a deep curve. To
straighten that line to bar-tight would take 74 tons in this case,
and long before that the towed ship would begin to move,

thus maintaining the curve or sag. About 25-30 tons is the estimated weight required to straighten a line when a 10,000 ton ship is taken in tow.

Anglers will understand this more readily when they appreciate that to land a 20-pound salmon they would require only a six- or seven-pound line, the spring of the rod taking the rest of the strain. So with *Turmoil* and her elaborate winch. When the strain begins to pull the tow wire bar-tight the winch automatically pays out line and retrieves it when the strain relaxes.

It is as much a question of overcoming initial inertia and keeping the body moving, as when a garage hand puts his back against a half-ton motor car, moves it and keeps it moving.

Turmoil had therefore been keeping *Flying Enterprise* moving at nearly four knots with a strain of not more than 30 tons on the register of her winch; most of the time it was only 20-22 tons.

"Operations still suspended due to weather. Alternative plan is to pass loop at end of towing wire to stern which is drier and now more accessible than the bow. Next attempt early morning if weather permits."

In the meantime Captain Parker on *Turmoil* had been studying the problem from another angle. He had realized that the two men were risking their lives every time they went on the bow or stern of the ship but as they were prepared to take that chance he was willing to co-operate.

A short radio conference was held between Carlsen, Parker and the destroyer and an alternative was contemplated, and one which could have been carried out in bad weather.

In brief, it was discussed whether Carlsen and Dancy could lower the *Flying Enterprise's* cable and anchor, allowing them to dangle below the ship, and the destroyer and tug would between them tow a wire beneath her and would attempt to pick up the hanging cable.

It has been done before, and is in fact a recognized

manœuvre, but if it failed, and it is by no means so simple as it reads, *Flying Enterprise*, already down by the head and drifting, would have the increased burden of the hanging cable and anchor. It was finally abandoned.

And *Flying Enterprise* drifted on.

Although the destroyer's despatches are terse and down to bare essentials, *Turmoil's* towing report—the extracts from her captain's log—are laconic almost to the point of being hairline.

"Jan. 3rd, 0800. Saw *Mactra* secured in inner harbour in charge of local tugs. Sailed to contact *Flying Enterprise*." That is Parker's first entry.

There are two more short references to making contact with the *John W. Weeks,* then the log reads: "Close to casualty 2324. Very close to casualty 2400."

That was on the night of January 3rd.

Through that night Parker kept the *Turmoil* near *Flying Enterprise*, studying the "casualty", as he always describes her, and there are hourly references: "Close to casualty." "Very close to casualty."

There is an unusual burst of literary excursion opposite the time 0920, on the morning of the 4th:

"Made several attempts to pick up buoy floated down from *Flying Enterprise*."

"0950. Failed."

Was ever a gallant attempt, even a gallant failure, dismissed in shorter terms? From the more descriptive dispatches of the *John W. Weeks* we know that *Turmoil* twisted and backed and filled only feet away from the *Flying Enterprise* trying to pick up that line.

To elaborate a little on that last entry, it meant that Parker kept his tug close to the wallowing "casualty" for half an hour, so close that one of her sudden, unpredictable lurches could have either thrown the *Flying Enterprise* over on to *Turmoil*, or *Turmoil* could have been hurled over on to the ship. Either would have spelled disaster with a capital D.

There are more laconic entries and austere references to the weather. A snarling wind and a rising sea are briefly dismissed: "Wind N.W. Force 5/6. Heavy swell."

Then comes an entry which for sheer brevity must be awarded the palm.

"1430. MR. DANCY WENT ABOARD CASUALTY."

From nine o'clock in the morning until mid-afternoon *Turmoil* and *Flying Enterprise* had been bobbing and curtseying to each other in a breath-taking dance with disaster waiting in the wings anxious to join in.

The only way to close *Flying Enterprise* was towards the side which was tilted heavily over into the water. No man could have lived on the smooth, wind- and water-lashed topside.

Flying Enterprise would swing round in a deadly lurch, dip her boat deck and port side under, would lash the water with davits and her masts would threaten to smack down on the sea.

Carlsen scrambled about on the ship like a cat on a hot tin roof, first to the bow, then to the stern, in successive attempts to make fast a tow so *Turmoil* would nudge in, timing her close approach so that she could gain a few precious feet to lighten the load that would inevitably fall on Carlsen when he tried to haul the tows aboard.

There were occasions when *Flying Enterprise*, with water white under her side, would swoop towards *Turmoil*. The tug would back away a little like a pugnacious terrier retreating from the lowering head of an angry bull, only to dart in again when the opportunity occurred.

And this went on for hours with Carlsen getting more weary with each attempt.

Then: "Mr. Dancy went aboard casualty."

Superb in its brevity, and superb in its execution.

Dancy's description of it is equally devoid of any heroics.

"Captain Parker did not tell me to jump to *Flying Enterprise*; he didn't tell anyone. I expect he thought it was suicidal.

"But everyone knew that he hoped that somehow somebody would make it, to help poor Carlsen struggling one-handed with the ropes.

"I was aft supervising the handling of some ropes as we manœuvred close to the stern of the *Enterprise* and I could see Carlsen there, on his own . . .

"Sometimes he would wave.

"The seas were pretty high, more than 20 feet at times.

"Suddenly there was a bang as the two ships crashed together. I knew that was my chance to do what Captain Parker would not ask any man to do, but was what he wanted. I took a long step across as the two ship hung together for a moment. As I reached *Flying Enterprise* they reeled apart, but Carlsen was no longer on his own.

"Then I realized that I hadn't got a life jacket on. Carlsen, who was wearing one, scrambled to meet me. We hung on with one hand, grinned at each other and shook hands.

"For hours we tried without success to get a line fast and when it was nearly dark we decided to wait."

(Dancy does not relate that there was one moment, when after herculean efforts they had dragged aboard a 3½-inch rope messenger which was followed by an 8-inch rope messenger and that was only inches away from success when the sea whirled the two ships apart, turning near success into heart-breaking failure.)

"Because I hadn't a life jacket Carlsen searched for one for me. He could only find one for a child, but I put it on."

That was how Mr. Dancy "went aboard casualty".

Captain Parker's next entry in his log was: "One indented plate in ship's stern where she banged against casualty."

We know that the men rested through the night with *Turmoil* and the destroyer in close attendance.

We know that the weather, playing at cat-and-mouse, had eased a little by the morning. We know that *Turmoil* seized on such an opportunity, closed in, and a tow was passed.

The log reads: "Jan 5. 0937. All fast." "1005. 150 fathoms

of 5-inch towing pendant paid out, 350 fathoms of 5½-inch wire paid out. 60 revolutions, speed 4 knots."

Through the successive days *Turmoil* nursed along her "casualty", reducing engine revolutions by five a minute reducing speed to three knots. When the sea and wind permitted the revolutions and speed would be increased again.

So it went on, and how Parker must have longed to give his tug full power!

There are log entries which illustrate, if only briefly, the problems involved.

By now the word "tow" had replaced "casualty". And in the entries it says: "Tow sheering from quarter to quarter, from three to four points on the starboard quarter to similar angle on the port quarter."

Remember the simile of the small boy and his kite in an earlier chapter?

Here was *Flying Enterprise*, the "casualty", the "tow", doing that and doing it with a vengeance. From being a more or less docile tow out on the starboard quarter she would suddenly start a lurching swing, an irresistible surge which would threaten to pull tight the vital tow.

While she was travelling forward a couple of hundred yards she would swoop through an arc of three or four times that distance, lie passive out on that quarter until another capricious sea would catch her off balance and would send her swinging away in another wild swoop.

That was something *Turmoil* could understand and could cope with. *Flying Enterprise* had ceased to be the "casualty" and had become the "tow". And as a "tow" she could be gently disciplined, could be allowed a little latitude, but in the main would be towed in a given direction.

And towed she was for 250 miles, each mile presenting its own problem, each problem being solved as it arose.

The cat-and-mouse act by the sea and the wind developed a deeper snarl. It was no longer a gentle pawing with the claws half concealed.

The Atlantic was moving in for its kill.

It chose the Indian hour, that hour in the day when men lower their guards momentarily, that moment when, wearied from the efforts of the past day, they relax for just the space of three long breaths before drawing on a reserve to meet the day which is to come.

"Wed. Jan. 9. 0130. Wind N.N.W. Force 4/5. Heavy swell. Tow parted."

There, once again, are the stage directions before the actors leap to frenzied action.

". . . Tow parted."

Equally terse are the brief entries in the log for the next few hours.

Because *Flying Enterprise* was rolling badly and was being swept by heavy seas it was considered too risky for the two men aboard her to try to connect a tow again.

She was drifting in the general direction she was intended to go so the demands were made on patience—and that was there in almost immeasurable quantities.

"0945: standing by."

"1200: standing by."

"1600: standing by."

Nine little groups of figures and words which cover nearly eleven hours of exasperation, of frustration—of wearying in-activity; eleven hours in which tremendous will-power was demanded from the tired-eyed men who waited and watched on tug and tow.

Once more ominous darkness shrouded the stage, but this time *Flying Enterprise* was loose, drifting slowly up-Channel.

Occasionally the wind would catch her when she was poised on the summit of a sea and she would lurch drunkenly sideways.

Parker, on *Turmoil*, the commanding officer of the destroyer, and the two men aboard *Flying Enterprise* knew, without admit-ting it in just so many words, that the freighter was getting more sluggish in her movements. She was showing a great weariness in the struggle.

U.S. destroyer closes in to pass hot coffee

Flying Enterprise takes a sheer out to starboard

"Tow's parted", and battered *Flying Enterprise* takes a 70 degree list

The end draws near. A 90 degree list and Carlsen and Dancy crouch
on the smoke stack ready to jump

"Jan. 9. 2000. All life-saving gear ready."

But *Flying Enterprise* was by no means beaten yet.

On through the night she plunged and as her stubbornness increased so the Atlantic unleashed a greater fury.

Dawn found the *Turmoil* closing in. Her log readings through the night were merely references to the wind, weather and visibility, and the terse entries: "Standing by . . . close to *F.E.* . . ." Once or twice there is the entry: "Very close to *F.E.*" Parker had closed in during momentary easing of the weather, knowing that often in a gale there comes a brief period of lifting pressure, a brief period which tantalizes and taunts only to deceive before the wind roars in with greater fury.

"Thurs. Jan 10. 0800. Wind to gale force. *F.E.*'s list seems to have increased."

"No longer was the ship the impersonal "casualty" or the "tow" to Parker. Probably quite unconsciously he had endowed her with a certain degree of personality.

His Chief Officer was on board her, his admiration for Carlsen had increased every hour from the time of his first contact with her, the ship herself had come near to endearing herself to him.

She had become not only *Flying Enterprise* to him, but *F.E.*, a term of affection almost.

The wind slashed and roared at her, the seas climbed over almost unceasingly as the little cavalcade drifted along roughly north-eastwards.

"1400. *F.E.*'s condition deteriorating. Lower in water and losing buoyancy."

"1430: *F.E.* listing badly. Port wing of bridge now under water. Standing by close to life-saving appliances in final degree of readiness."

Now it was a question of saving life. All thoughts of towing were wiped away.

Turmoil was so close to *Flying Enterprise* that the sea, crashing over her and turning into lashing spray, was whipping across *Turmoil's* bridge in blinding showers.

H

"1445 : *F.E.* now foundering. Captain Carlsen signalled his readiness to abandon ship by climbing on high side and waving his arm."

"1510: Wind, whole gale, westerly. Captain Carlsen, accompanied by Mr. Dancy, scrambled along end of smoke-stack and prepared to jump."

"1522. Jumped."

"1531. Both men recovered from water and attended to."

"1540. Altered course and proceeded to Falmouth."

"1630. Received signal from *Dexterous*. *F.E.* foundered 1611."

In eight words Captain Parker described an operation which seamen who saw it, from the American destroyer, from the lifeboats which by then were out, from her companion ship, *Dexterous*, and from the decks of other ships which had newspaper men and cameramen aboard, describe as a superb piece of seamanship.

And by one of those curious ironic twists that life holds for all of us *Turmoil's* captain and crew, Mr. Dancy and Captain Carlsen were not to see the final plunge of the ship for which they had fought so long and so resolutely.

"Altered course and proceeded to Falmouth." And fifty minutes after that came the signal:

"*Flying Enterprise* has gone down."

CHAPTER TEN

HER closing minutes must not be dismissed in quite such a laconic manner.

Dancy and Carlsen both knew that their fight to save the ship was coming to an end, although neither said so in words for some time after they had realized it.

"Both of us sat gazing at the bulkhead, which was where the deckhead ought to be," Dancy relates.

"I was watching the curtains, and they were slowly but surely moving towards the deckhead (that is, to an angle of more than 80 degrees).

"I shinned up the rope" [previously fixed by them to enable them to get out quickly] "took a look round and returned to the captain. He climbed out and had a look, too.

"Then he said: 'I think it is time for us to go.' We talked it over and we decided that the best place was the funnel, now lying almost flat.

"We went out there and sat down. The underside of the funnel was dipping under water and sometimes the water came up to our feet. Up to then we had hoped that a helicopter would be coming out to pick us off so we sat and waited. We didn't talk much.

"Then we saw a message being flashed from the destroyer, and we read it together in silence. It was to say that the weather was too bad for the helicopter to rescue us."

Turmoil, too, received this signal and moved in immediately. *Flying Enterprise* by now was like a huge whale thrashing away in its death throes. Somewhere under the water were her two masts; possibly her derricks had broken partly free and were plunging about just beneath the surface like huge harpoons.

Parker came to a snap decision.

To *Dexterous* he signalled: "I am going in for them. Stand by me in case there is trouble."

Trouble there might easily have been, too. *Flying Enterprise* was still capable of lifting herself partly from the water and producing one of her gigantic swooping lurches. She might easily have reared up, corkscrewed over and demolished *Turmoil*.

The tug could easily have had her screws caught up in the welter of rigging, wire stays, and other debris lashing around, and with her screws immobilized she would have been as helpless as *Flying Enterprise*.

Parker kept his eyes on the two tiny figures crouched on the horizontal funnel.

Carefully, exquisitely, like a bullfighter moving in, he nursed *Turmoil* closer.

"They're going in!" Half a dozen voices on *Turmoil* rapped it out as the two men slipped into the water, but Parker had seen them.

With but one brief glance to see that *Dexterous* was handy —and she was—he closed up to the two heads in the water.

And in a few minutes—nine, to be exact—from the time they had jumped they were safely on deck.

From *Dexterous* came a signal: "Good show!"

Dancy tells: "Carlsen and I stood up. He looked at me and I knew he wanted me to go first. So I did."

Thus was a nicety of the sea observed. The captain *was* the last to leave his doomed ship.

"He came up beside me," Dancy goes on, "and I said: 'Bad luck, Captain,' and he replied: 'Never mind; it couldn't be helped.'"

They had previously agreed to keep close together in the water if and when it became necessary to jump, and they floated side by side, hand in hand until *Turmoil* loomed up and they were hauled aboard.

As *Turmoil* backed away, making her triumphant signal: "Both picked up", *Flying Enterprise* lurched and sank deeper in the water.

Carlsen stood alone on the deck of *Turmoil* for a few

minutes looking towards his doomed ship, his face drawn with weariness, water dripping from him, but his shoulders were squared.

Then he turned without a word and entered a cabin where dry clothes and attention waited for him.

Turmoil's engines started to throb powerfully and she was ten miles or more away when one of *Turmoil's* radio operators got the message from *Dexterous.* "*Flying Enterprise* has sunk."

Turmoil had disappeared into the murk of the tail end of the blow when *Flying Enterprise's* last moments came. By now only her bow was above water; around her lay the mass of debris.

Momentarily the bow climbed perpendicularly as if coming to attention for a last salute. The sirens of the ships round her—the destroyer, the *Dexterous,* the *Abeille 25,* and the small host of ships which had taken newspaper men and cameramen out to the scene—sounded their shrill, mournful farewell, a last call to a gallant ship.

And soon only the debris remained.

With that cruel twist which is such a part of the sea, before darkness set in the wind dropped, the sea was just an uneasy, oily swell, and over the western ocean a pale yellow sun shone coldly from under gold-flecked clouds, lighting the stage before leaving the world to darkness—and to defeat.

It was only right that Carlsen should not see the final moments of the ship with which he fought.

Some may attack this as sheer sentimentality. A ship, they may argue, is just an engined steel box, a purely commercial proposition.

That is as it may be. Either one understands or one does not, and argument for or against is futile because both protagonists are set in their views.

Commercialism there was, of course. But one can admire a fight even if it is fought out in the circle of moneymaking.

The world can watch with admiration a man bucking the stock market and cleaning up a million. The world can sympathize if he loses and goes to the wall, and reserves the right to say: "Well, it was a nice fight and he was a game fighter and a game loser."

It can say the same of Carlsen and of *Turmoil*.

All sorts of fantastic stories have been in circulation since of the vast fortune presumed to be hidden away in *Flying Enterprise*. Not for one moment do I believe there was any, but even had she been loaded down to the gunwales with solid gold bars it was still a grand fight.

Turmoil's owners got precisely nothing out of it. In fact they were considerably out-of-pocket because they undertook the tow of *Flying Enterprise* on the standard Lloyd's agreement: "No cure, no pay." Payment only if salvage is successfully completed.

So any picture of her owners getting a fat cheque for the abortive attempt is just so much sheer nonsense.

Equally absurd would be any vision of Captain Parker and his crew rubbing their hands gleefully and saying: "Fifty miles more to go and we are in the money."

They are on pay just as any other ship sailing under the Red Ensign, no matter how valuable its cargo.

It is true that the owners of the *Flying Enterprise* did award Captain Parker, Mr. Dancy and the crew of *Turmoil* a sum of money, but that was an expression of their admiration, not a commercial assessment of the task attempted.

A garage mechanic does not get a vast sum merely because the broken-down car he goes out to tow is a silver-plated Rolls Royce. To him it is a broken-down car and he is on a weekly rate of pay for dealing with any type of car.

Here it is in cold, hard figures.

In her fight to rescue *Flying Enterprise*, *Turmoil* steamed 676 miles and her steaming time was 139 hours at an average speed of 4.08 knots.

Flying Enterprise drifted 139 miles from the time *Turmoil* made contact; she was towed 250 miles and altogether they covered 815 miles.

To do that *Turmoil* used up 26 tons of fuel oil, lost a considerable amount of expensive towing gear, and fired upwards of more than a dozen line-carrying rockets.

And all for nothing. That is just the luck of the game.

How valuable would have been that twelve to fifteen hours lost at the beginning!

Turmoil and *Flying Enterprise* might conceivably have missed the full weight of that last N.N.W. gale, would have had some shelter from the long toe of England thrust out into the Atlantic and the tow would not have parted until smoother water was reached. Putting another tow aboard, with the two resolute men on her, would have been comparatively child's play.

It was not to be.

Now let us examine quite cold-bloodedly what some self-appointed critics of the entire operation have been dogmatic and opinionated enough to describe as the serious delay between the *Flying Enterprise* first striking trouble and her being taken in tow.

This is not a defence of *Turmoil*, or of any other tug. That is not necessary, neither am I qualified by any inside knowledge or technical experience to attempt a defence.

It is an examination of all the known facts, details of which are available for anybody who can read, or who cares to refresh his memory by re-reading the story of *Turmoil* and *Flying Enterprise* once again.

One self-appointed critic, writing from the security of London, for a weekly paper of strictly limited circulation, produced this ponderous—and preposterous—critique:

"The authorities are gravely concerned over the lack of towing facilities available immediately it was known that *Flying Enterprise* was in difficulties at a spot not more than a day's sailing time from British ports.

"They are anxious to know why no tug sailed until the doomed ship had been drifting for nine days without assistance."

Well, let's tackle that one first.

Who are the "authorities" so vaguely mentioned?

Lloyds? There is no evidence that they were more deeply concerned than to pass messages of the state of the ship, her position as received, and to transmit any other messages required of them.

The Ministry of Transport (Shipping) or some other vague Whitehall body?

Had there been any necessity for an inquiry into *Turmoil's* towing, had it been barely more than whispered that any neglect on the part of her Master had caused or contributed to the loss of the freighter, then there would have been a court of Inquiry under the Shipping Act of 1894 with legal and expert assessors probing into every act, every movement, every moment of the tow, and into everything that happened before, during and after, "without fear or favour".

So what authorities are (or were) gravely concerned at the lack of towing facilities available?

There are one or two similar criticisms equally vaguely cloaked and in one is embodied what I imagine is intended to be a brilliant gem of constructive thinking. The critic offers the suggestion that tugs should be kept at certain ports with steam up and be available at immediate notice so that they can dash forth at once to any ship which signals that she is in distress.

Truly a glimpse of the obvious—40 years late.

To-day, now, at the moment you are reading this there are at various places on the eastern Atlantic coastline, ranging from Azores to Iceland, taking in Gibraltar, Vigo, Brest, Falmouth, Cork, the Clyde and Kirkwall, possibly a dozen or more powerful tugs belonging to acutely competitive towing and salvage concerns, all ready to sail at the drop of a hat (or the receipt of a terse signal—which is the same thing to them).

Those tugs cost upwards of £50,000 a year to maintain —probably more—and if their owners relied solely on the possibility of salvage coming their way they would shortly be setting course for Carey Street, London, W.C., to that grim little court to which men come who have spent more than they have earned.

Those ships earn their bread and butter by the mundane task of towing, not merely from one dock to another but often across the world.

In the past two or three years *Turmoil* has towed, among other things, a grain elevator one hundred feet high, sticking up out of the sea like a portion of Blackpool's celebrated tower, from Bristol to Liverpool. She has towed a brand new ferry ship twice as long as herself from this country to Istanbul in Turkey, and has towed a French troopship from Aden to Marseilles, and two obsolete tankers in one tow from Curaçao to Antwerp.

She and her companions, the *Dexterous* and *Medina*, also towed some of those tragic German scuttled warships from Scapa Flow to the last ignominy of the breaker's yard.

Towage, the daily round, the common task. And the deep-sea tugs belonging to the other companies do the same. When their tow is complete they return to the station of their choice and wait—for another tow, or for a call from a distressed ship.

In this instance, that of the *Flying Enterprise*, *Turmoil* was not the first tug called and sent to her. *Turmoil*, as we have seen, was committed to the Anglo-Saxon ship the *Mactra*, which had got into trouble in the same hurricane which smote *Flying Enterprise*.

By a tragic sequence of events other tugs stationed in the area were heavily committed.

It was arranged that the Dutch deep-sea tug *Oceaan* should proceed to *Flying Enterprise* and she was actually doing so when she received an urgent call from her sister tug the *Zwarte Zee*, struggling with a large tow in the Bay of Biscay. It was a call as urgent as the *Flying Enterprise*. Her sister tug was in trouble, and looming up to leeward was the dread French coast.

Oceaan altered course to assist. And *Flying Enterprise* had to battle on alone.

So the gem of constructive criticism develops leaks, besides being about forty years behind the times.

There were tugs on station, there were tugs available, but just at that moment they were all heavily committed.

It was tragic, but there it was.

What justification was there for sending tugs from Gibraltar, or the Clyde, or the Azores, to *Flying Enterprise*, which was threatening to founder at any moment, anyway, with a list of 60 degrees—a list which still puzzles real experts? How did she stay afloat so long with it?

On this point, tugs have sailed as many miles to answer an SOS, only to find that their long slam through terrible weather has been abortive.

There are certain ships, sailing under a certain national flag, which seem to live a hairs-breadth from the same degree of ready hysteria as the housewife who upsets some fat over her stove and when the flames roar upwards sends for the fire brigade, the ambulance, the police—and all her neighbours.

More than once a powerful and expensive salvage tug has slammed through a gale over a couple of hundred miles or more on receipt of a distress signal from one such ship, only to find that the cargo has shifted (it more often than not being grain and the Master having skimped on shifting boards to get more aboard). When daylight arrives and a ten degree list does not seem so alarming the tug has been asked to stand by until weather moderates.

On a "No cure, no pay" basis that proves expensive.

But the tugs still sail, slipping their moorings and sliding from harbour in no more time than it takes to get a car out of a suburban garage.

One wonders what the critics would have done if faced by the set of circumstances which prevailed between December 27th and January 3rd when *Turmoil* sailed to contact *Flying Enterprise*.

Would they, one wonders, have ordered *Turmoil* to slip her tow on *Mactra*, which was, remember, a "casualty" off

Fastnet Rock? Or would they have ordered *Oceaan* to disregard the urgent call for help from her sister tug?

Having given such resolute orders one then goes on to ponder what the situation would have been had *Flying Enterprise* foundered.

There would have been *Mactra*, still a "casualty" drifting closer to the rock-bound Irish coast, there would have been a Dutch tug, in difficulties with a tow close to the French coast, and *Turmoil* and the *Oceaan* both standing by a sinking *Flying Enterprise*.

Even had *Flying Enterprise* remained afloat, as she did, the same situation would have arisen.

I have yet to learn that the Americans are backward in offering full-blooded criticism. They are nationals who have grown up in the tenets of free speech, in a country where they can stand up and slang the President himself, and all he can do is to answer back in similar vein—or go off and play golf.

In the thousands of words transmitted by the destroyers *John W. Weeks* and *Willard Keith* there is not one word of criticism of Parker and *Turmoil* or any suggestion that rescue tugs were dilatory in coming along.

They knew, from seaman up to Admiral Carney, that all that could be done was done to the best of men's ability.

Through the story of *Turmoil's* efforts to get a tow aboard, after she got the tow aboard, and after it broke, there are references to the French tug *Abeille 25* standing by.

Now, why did not the French tug close up, put a tow aboard and help to increase the towing speed?

The best man to answer that is Captain Huido, the Master of the *Abeille 25*.

There was more than ample power available in *Turmoil* to tow *Flying Enterprise*, he stated. Had the ship been towed any faster there would have been considerable risk of her turning over and going down. He added that had he been fast to *Flying Enterprise* he would have done exactly what Parker did on *Turmoil*, i.e., set course for Falmouth, at the same towing speed, 3 to 3½ knots.

The problem, he explained, was not towing. It was the condition of the towed ship, and the fact that there were only two men aboard her to attempt to handle the heavy tows in bad weather. He estimated that it would require five or six men aboard to do it properly and to watch the tow through day and night.

No doubt had Parker felt that another tug would have been of use he would have called on *Abeille 25* because his owners and the *Abeille* owners are associate companies.

So it resolves itself to the simple fact that the Atlantic had won a battle, as it has won others, and will go on winning.

Somewhere along the line, nobody knows where, there had been an error of omission or commission, and *Flying Enterprise* had paid the price.

The debris from *Flying Enterprise* was still floating forlornly on the waters when *Turmoil* slipped out of Falmouth, bound for Liverpool to take a tow to Holland.

Once more she was on the common round, the daily task.

CHAPTER ELEVEN

THE world knows in detail the story of the fight to save the *Flying Enterprise*.

It is worth recounting how it got to know the story through the Press.

When any item of news on shore becomes of national interest it is not difficult to obtain. There are local men who have information and sources of obtaining it at their finger-tips and when a national newspaper deems it of sufficient importance it will amplify the local man's powers by sending down a man from London.

When the story happens at sea it is a different problem.

The men involved on the ships have far too much to do to spend time elaborating for newspaper men the task they have on hand.

The brief facts that a ship is in trouble, the extent of her trouble and her position are sent out by Lloyds and is an extract from the ship's report.

But they are just the bare bones.

When disaster first hit *Flying Enterprise* she was but one of a number of ships appearing in that purple-inked duplicated list of maritime casualties sent out to all newspapers by Lloyds.

It was worth a mention, to be included in the overall story of the mighty gale which had brought down telephone wires, blown off roofs and had started several ships asking for assistance. Two paragraphs were dilated to half a dozen when it was learned that two ships had successfully rescued the crew and passengers.

Then came the short, terse information that *Flying Enterprise's* captain, name not then known, had refused to leave his ship, over on her beam ends and drifting in the gale.

Fleet Street sat up and took notice.

Newspaper men, despite the hysterical claims of people who when in doubt attack the Press, are not ghouls. They prefer reporting either the mundane, and doing a sound job, or retailing romance. But when disaster strikes with equal competence they report that. And note that they REPORT it as it happens, not comment on it.

What was being done about taking the ship in tow?

The owners reassuringly said a powerful tug was on its way and even if it failed to get the ship in it would undoubtedly take off the Master.

When he landed he would be worth a story, Fleet Street reasoned, and local men on the coast were alerted to watch for the return of the tug.

The sequence of events is now known. Carlsen was in there battling alone. He had become a figure of more than passing interest.

National newspapers do not hesitate one moment over the expense of reaching the scene of any affair of importance. Trains, cars, aircraft, ships—any means of conveyance—are used regardless of the comfort of their reporters or amount of money involved so long as they contribute to getting the facts and getting them quickly, whether they be the written word or a photograph.

But *Flying Enterprise* was several hundred miles out from Land's End in visibility at times down to only a few hundred yards.

Nobody quite knew where she was or what was happening.

To every newspaper man worth his salt at certain times in his career there comes a hunch which he follows and it leads him to that success which he likes to remember when subsequent failures loom large.

Jock Drummond, now Picture Editor of *Picture Post*, was at that time head of the Kemsley newspapers photographic department, and following a sudden hunch he obtained for the *Daily Graphic*, and other Kemsley newspapers, a satisfying scoop.

He knew that an American destroyer, the *John W. Weeks*, was hammering out from Plymouth towards the *Flying Enterprise*, but she had already sailed.

Having served in the Navy during the war, he was familiar with the problem of drift and the power of the sea.

Every newspaper is as well equipped with up-to-date charts as any merchant ship. There was a brief conference of ex-naval men on his staff over one such chart, *Flying Enterprise's* last known position was marked, the direction of the wind was estimated and a cross was made.

Then Drummond followed up his hunch. He rang the Air Ministry to ask if any aircraft of Coastal Command would be doing any "search and fix" exercises in that area, and if so could he send along a photographer and a reporter.

There was such an exercise due to start and the two men could go.

The hunch paid off. There, in the sea away to the south-west, was a ready-made target for a "search and fix" exercise, and Stanley Devon, the photographer, with William Courtney, then the *Graphic* Air Correspondent, flew over *Flying Enterprise*.

The *Daily Graphic* had scooped the pool by one whole day.

It was one of the photographs taken by Devon that confirmed the then doubtful fact that Carlsen was still alive and on *Flying Enterprise*.

The rest of the national newspapers were on the trail of the *Graphic* scoop with every ounce of energy and ingenuity they could devise.

They could never hope to catch up on that precious twenty-four hours, of course, but from then onwards they could give the story complete saturation coverage.

To watch a specialized organization like a national newspaper go into action to give such coverage is a thrilling spectacle even to men who have worked at it for years and are hardened to it.

So far as Fleet Street is concerned, there is none of the semi-hysteria with which Hollywood has endowed newspaper work. Every possible source of information is tackled by telephone and by personal contact, and as the story flows into the office, often changing its form a dozen times in an hour, skilled men appraise, reject or accept parts of it and, working against the clock, knit it into the ultimate which is what you read at your breakfast table. And it is all done with an almost uncanny lack of noise and shouting.

The *Daily Mail, Daily Express, News Chronicle, Daily Mirror, Daily Telegraph,* the *Daily Herald* and the agencies, both British and American, were by now in full cry on the story.

There was no question of the Air Ministry having given Drummond and the *Graphic* an unfair advantage.

He alone had asked for the facility and had been granted it. Had any other paper made the request that, too, would have been given similar facilities.

Fleet Street knows the rules and abides by them.

Eventually there was another exercise—note that no special flights were laid on by the Air Ministry; they were normal "search and fix" exercises and as 29 newspapers and news agencies wanted to go a selection was made on the usual rota system adopted by Ministries and newspapers. A section should work for the whole.

So on the second trip the *Daily Mail, Daily Express, News Chronicle,* the *Daily Herald,* the *Yorkshire Post,* the *Daily Mirror,* Associated Press, TV Newsreel and Gaumont-British News were allocated seats on Lancasters.

An adequate coverage as all newspapers share pictures and coverage on a rota job.

Perhaps the first stunning impact of *Flying Enterprise's* plight was thrust home on the British public by a huge picture, taking up more than half of the front page, in the *Daily Express.*

It slammed home to millions of readers as they dealt with their breakfasts, or swung in trains and buses that morning: "Here is a ship, a heroic ship and on her is a heroic man."

It was the beginning of a story which never shrunk in size up to its last minutes.

Mr. Davies, Second Matc of *Turmoil*, fires line carrying pistol

Kenneth Dancy and Captain Dan Parker autograph a bottle of 'Bubbly'

Somewhere out there is the *Casualty*

"And there she is . . ."

In addition to the flights, newspaper men were on their way by sea—into a snarling gale, remember, sailing in cockleshell craft.

John May, of the *Daily Express*, Howard Johnson of the *Daily Mirror* and L. E. W. Heath of the *Daily Telegraph* had cajoled, almost hypnotized, boat owners into putting to sea and there was a stern race between them. No quarter given and none asked—and the devil take the hindmost.

Both John May and Howard Johnson have since bemoaned to me the fact that they could not persuade their boat owners to close in to *Flying Enterprise* enough to enable them to jump aboard. Otherwise Dancy's famous leap would have been duplicated twice over.

But Carlsen waved them away. A lurch from *Flying Enterprise* would have overwhelmed them, game as they were to try.

The story was too big for any one man to handle—there were too many ends. The only source of first-hand information was the destroyer *John W. Weeks* and later the *Willard Keith*.

And this is where one must congratulate the United States Navy in this country.

It told the world. This is how it did it.

The destroyers signalled all information to United States headquarters in North Audley Street, London, W.1, where the American Navy set up a Press Headquarters.

Representatives of every national newspaper, the London representatives of larger provincial papers, the United Press, the Associated Press, International News Service, the Press Association and other bodies moved in, at the invitation of the U.S. Navy.

The United States Navy has always been Public Relations conscious, and in fact in that Press Office has a notice which adjures: "Information is the key to good relations with your community; a Command responsibility, an individual responsibility."

Rear-Admiral Walter Boone, then commanding U.S. Navy

I

in the Eastern Atlantic, took the task over with his staff, and treated it as a major operation, as indeed it was.

To two of his men he delegated the task of seeing that everything that happened out in the Atlantic, so far as the destroyers knew, would be retailed in detail first from Commander Thompson and later from Commander O'Brien, the captains of the destroyers.

The two men who took over the task were Lieutenant James Martin, a regular naval officer from Passiac, New Jersey, a Public Relations specialist, and Petty Officer Kenneth Barnsdale, from Charlotte, North Carolina.

Barnsdale, an ex-reporter and Canadian-born, put in almost 60 hours in an unbroken stretch and Martin was absent for only short periods.

As the destroyers' signals came in they were duplicated and handed out immediately, and telephones all over the building were allocated to newspaper men.

Admiral Boone and his senior staff officers, too, had their copies and suggested that Thompson and O'Brien should try to get a little imagery into their reports.

How they succeeded is now known and the stories of Carlsen's use of the butter to reduce chafe, his interchange of messages with his parents, and of his famous plum cake, were highlights in the sterner narrative.

The efforts of the destroyers to get close enough to pass hot food and other material had to be dragged out of Commander Thompson and Commander O'Brien, but dragged out they were.

As the hours lengthened into days there was hot coffee made available at U.S. Headquarters and by "private arrangements" also hot dogs!

A reflection of the cordiality, almost affection, that sprang up between the horde of newspaper men at U.S. headquarters and Lieut. James Martin and Petty Officer Barnsdale is that long before the story was ended they had become "Jim" and "Barney". Newspaper men are not given easily to granting affectionate abbreviations of names. They have to be earned. And earned they well and truly were.

Should "Jim" Martin and "Barney" Barnsdale ever read this they will know that they are still remembered with regard, affection and a deep respect for a job well done.

All the national newspapers gave the *Flying Enterprise* story complete saturation coverage after the initial jolt administered through Drummond's hunch and scoop.

How much a coverage can be assessed by the fact that in most newspaper libraries, where everything is filed away, a dozen large envelopes hold the cuttings of the story and not many news stories go beyond two or three envelopes.

One or two people have expressed some discontent at the fact that Parker on *Turmoil* declined to elaborate his efforts while he was making them.

But in the main the newspapers realized that he had only a small crew, his radio operators were on twenty-four-hour watch and he had neither the men to spare to cope with the requests, nor the time.

Similarly disgruntled attacks have been made on the management of Overseas Towage and Salvage for not issuing more detailed information.

Mr. Andrews, the managing director, and Major Mill, his personal assistant, were at Falmouth arranging berthing facilities for *Flying Enterprise* if the tow was successful. They were much too busy on a vital task to spare time to discuss something of which they knew but little anyway.

They could quite easily have taken a boat out to *Turmoil*. They declined, partly because they were busy the clock round twice, and partly because they knew that all that could be done by Parker was being done.

So that is how the world was told the story of *Turmoil's* gallant, if unsuccessful, attempt to save the *Flying Enterprise*, was told of the inexhaustible courage of Captain Kurt Carlsen, and of Dancy's leap to join him.

An adequate story by any yardstick.

CHAPTER TWELVE

THE emphasis, up to now, has been on the rescue and salvage work of the deep-sea tugs. But towing is not without its drama, even its tragedy.

From the dry legal phrases of the findings of the formal investigation held into the loss of the Brazilian ex-battleship *São Paulo* on or about November 4th, 1951, it is possible to reconstruct in more dramatic detail the long tow of forty-five days, culminating in that tense hour when the two towing tugs, threatened themselves by danger, were parted from the battleship in a near-hurricane—and she was never seen again.

The inquiry was held at 10, Carlton House Terrace, London, S.W.1, on the 4th, 5th, 6th, 7th and 8th days of October, 1954, before Mr. R. F. Hayward, Q.C., assisted by Captain A. M. Atkinson and Mr. W. J. Nutton.

So that was a five-day exhaustive inquiry which probed every conceivable angle, every possible clue, in a search to find what had caused the foundering of the towed battleship.

Right away it must be stated that the Court completely cleared those responsible for the preparation of the *São Paulo* for her tow and those who did the towing.

It did so in these words:

The Court having inquired into the circumstances attending the above-mentioned shipping casualty (the loss of the *São Paulo* ex-battleship) finds the reasons stated in the Annex hereto, that the said ship probably foundered, either with or without capsizing, in a very heavy gale from the N.W. while in the trough of a very high sea, after the two tugs which had been towing her had parted their towing connections; that the sinking or capsizing was probably within an hour thereafter; and that the loss may have been caused or contributed to by the failure of the temporary closings of some gunports or other openings. The Court finds that there is no blame to be attributed to any of those concerned in the preparations for the towage or handling of the *São Paulo* at sea.

Dated this 14th day of October, 1954.

R. F. Hayward, Judge.

We concur in the above Report.

A. M. Atkinson ⎫
W. J. Nutton ⎬ (Assessors.)
          ⎭

For five days an eminent Q.C., sitting with men skilled in the sea, had inquired into every possible move that was made before the aged battleship was taken in tow, and into every move made during the tow until the fatal moment when the tow lines parted—and afterwards.

It was not the purpose of those worthy gentlemen to search for and produce highlights. They had but to find one answer. "WHY?" and if there was blame, justly apportion it, and if there was none, to say so.

It is impossible to read that report without sensing the gradually heightening drama culminating in tragedy.

The *São Paulo* was an aged battleship, almost a relic of bygone days. She was built in 1910 at Barrow-in-Furness by Vickers Armstrong in the days when navies reigned supreme, when ships which could carry guns throwing a shell weighing a ton for fifteen miles could be, and were, the key to all maritime warfare.

One can imagine the scene at Barrow-in-Furness the day she was launched. The Brazilian ambassador in London, glowing with pride, resplendent in top hat and frock coat, proudly escorting his lady, she handling her dainty parasol and sweeping skirt with practised ease, to the small green and white bunting-covered platform. She swings the bottle of champagne, it breaks in foam, in musical South American Spanish she says: "I name you *São Paulo*. May God preserve all who sail in you." And being a good Catholic she adds a prayer of her own to Mary the Mother of All.

Then a lunch with Brazilian and British naval officers in navy blue and shining gold, and the directors of the building firm toasting each other while the newly launched ship lies securely moored, sitting buoyantly in the debris-flecked water, the green ensign of Brazil crackling crisply at her stern.

A few miles away the restless sea waits to greet the initiate, waits with endless patience, waits to pass on its inevitable caution: "If there have been errors of omission or commission I will find them out. Be sure of that."

São Paulo sailed the seas, the proud flagship of the Brazilian navy, for thirty-six years—until 1946, when she was laid up in Rio de Janeiro.

She had lived through the First World War when big ships with big guns had held poised at their gun muzzles the winning or losing of a war in an afternoon; she had lived to see three British terriers, the cruisers *Ajax*, *Achilles* and *Exeter*, defeat and humiliate the *Graf Spee*, the pride of the German Navy, in another world war. She had lived to hear the pundits declare the death knell of the capital ship. Then she had lain alongside the quay—scrap iron for the highest bidder.

In August, 1951, she was bought by the British Iron and Steel Corporation (Salvage) Ltd., to be towed to Britain.

The inquiry elicited the information that she had last been dry docked in 1948 and was heavily coated with marine growth.

The inquiry posed the question: "What arrangements were made by the owners (The British Iron and Steel Corporation (Salvage), Ltd.), for the delivery of the *São Paulo* to Britain?

The answer was: "The Ensign Rigging Company, Ltd., were engaged to provide a runner crew for bringing the vessel under tow to the United Kingdom and to be responsible for her preparations for the voyage. The owners contracted with Metal Industries, Ltd., for her towage by the tug *Bustler*, and the latter firm sub-contracted with the Overseas Towage and

Salvage Company, Ltd., for an additional tug to assist, and the tug *Dexterous* was detailed for the work."

The *Bustler* is by now a more or less familiar figure. She was the first of the class built of which *Turmoil* is one. There might be minor differences, but in essence she is the same.

Dexterous, as quoted in the report, is an oil-fired tug of 600 tons, 147 feet in length, 33 feet beam, and with loaded draught of 13 feet forward and 17 feet aft. She is fitted with triple expansion engines developing 1,350 horsepower and is single-screwed. She has a steaming range of 28 days, and at a pinch was herself capable of towing *São Paulo*.

Now back to the report of the Court.

It states that a runner crew of nine men, including Mr. W. Painter, managing director of Ensign Rigging Company, and a Mr. Adams, his mate, arrived in Rio de Janeiro on August 25th and worked with energy, and dockyard labour started on September 5th. Altogether 3,691 man-hours were put in preparing her before the tow started on September 20th, 1951.

The terms "riggers" and "runners" are worth a little explanation. They go back to the days of the old sailing ships. Immediately a ship arrived in port her crew, probably with a thirst of considerable size, waited not on the order of their going but went forthwith as soon as they received their pay for the voyage.

But there were complicated tasks to be done. The sails had to be unbent and stowed, the wear and tear of the voyage on the rigging had to be repaired and it was done by shore riggers working as the ship was being discharged and loaded. Usually they were in charge of the Boss Rigger who took his orders from the Mate who was standing by the ship while she was in harbour.

That explains the term "rigger" now applied to the skeleton crews provided on steamships while they are in port, mainly for the purpose of moving her from one berth to another until a new crew is signed on.

Of course they do no actual rigging these days, but the term remains.

And from the same period comes the term "runner". A ship would perhaps discharge in one port and would be required to make a short run to another to load, or perhaps to dry dock for an overhaul.

A regular crew would not be signed on for that, but a temporary and skeleton crew would be shipped for the short "run".

They are terms which have come down through periods and remain because there are no better ones to make them obsolete.

So when a ship has to be moved from one harbour to another port, or when an inanimate tow has to be manned, contractors and shipping companies get into touch with a rigging company.

So it was with the *São Paulo.*

Mr. Painter had his men, all experienced seamen, and they worked on the ship, securing this and that, using their wide knowledge of the sea.

But the over-all master of the tow was Captain Jonathan Adam,[1] Master of the tug *Bustler.* Once the little cavalcade got to sea it was he who would have the final responsibility of saying nay or yea to any problem.

The amount of work done was enormous, and has no real part in this narrative except to show that deep-sea towage is not merely a matter of going alongside a ship, tying a thick rope to one end of her and moving off like a breakdown lorry with a damaged car.

Tug masters know their sea and its relentless and unforgiving moods.

Let us take a further extract from the report of the Court.

It runs: "There was some delay in preparing the ship, but eventually the work was done . . . In addition, the Masters and

[1] Captain Adam has since achieved the goal of most seamen. He has gone ashore and now has a farm in the Western Isles.

officers of the *Bustler* and *Dexterous* assisted, and also the Chief
Engineer of the *Bustler*.

"The Master of the *Bustler*, who in fact acted as towing
master, was concerned about the trim of the *São Paulo* and
carried out some ballasting operations by using *Bustler's* fire
pump and hoses into the tanks via manholes. The manhole
covers were screwed down by *Bustler's* Chief Officer and
carpenter. The Chief Engineer noted that the boilers were
empty . . . he was satisfied that all closures of shell fittings and
other vulnerable connections in the machinery spaces, except
in one instance of a six-inch overboard discharge, where the
lid had been removed and the valve displaced. This was
satisfactorily blanked off."

Finally *São Paulo* lay ready to tow.

With *Bustler* and *Dexterous* ahead, the towlines tightened,
the hulk began to move. And that was on September 20th,
1951.

Experienced men had prepared her for the voyage and to
the best of their knowledge they had left nothing undone.

On the *São Paulo* itself were eight men; one other, having
been injured on sailing day, had been left behind.

She was off with rather more than seventy days' towing
facing her.

Now picture the little cavalcade. The looming bulk of
São Paulo, with eight men on her, and the two tugs *Bustler* and
Dexterous, dwarfed against the ex-battleship, their sterns well
down, their screws biting sturdily into the water, making
progress.

What was the towing equipment for this long voyage?

Bustler used 100 fathoms of 22 inches manilla attached to
her 350 fathoms of 5 inches wire on to her electric towing
winch, which resists a pull of 39 tons and automatically
retrieves the wire after excessive strain.

In other words, the winch would do what the small boy
with a kite would do. It would give a little when extra strain
came and would adjust itself as the strain eased.

Dexterous used a double wire pennant from her towing hook to 70 fathoms of 10 inches nylon hawser and 230 fathoms of 5 inches wire.

These formidable tows were made fast to short lengths of anchor cable on *São Paulo*.

A fathom being six feet, the tugs were roughly a little more than 2,000 feet or more away from *São Paulo*, allowing for the sag in the tows.

In order to be able to communicate with one another the *São Paulo* was equipped with a walkie-talkie set which had been put in order and installed by *Bustler's* radio staff. It had a range of ten miles and arrangements were made for routine talks between 8 a.m. and 9 a.m. each morning and between 8 p.m. and 9 p.m. each evening.

Also, arrangements were made that *Bustler* or *São Paulo* would fly a flag by day or flash a light by night if either desired to communicate with the other.

And so they sailed in fine weather with little wind and sea, making slow but sure progress.

For 45 days the little flotilla plodded on. About October 19th and 20th it encountered strong north-easterly winds which went on until on November 4th it had become a gale which had raised a heavy sea which caused the ships to heave-to head to wind. It was a hazard which the experienced men on the tow had expected and for which they had prepared.

The tow master, Captain Adam, on *Bustler*, obviously watched his charge, constantly weighing the onslaught of the sea against his knowledge of what his tow would stand.

On *São Paulo* Mr. Painter was not idle.

Sometime during the morning of November 4th Mr. Painter reported to *Bustler*: "I have just completed a round and she is tight. The only sign of anything is that I am getting a slight trickle through my gunports." He added: "It is nothing."

But the sea waited and watched its chance. Without warning the *São Paulo* took a heavy sheer to starboard and fell into the trough of a sea, dragging the two tugs astern and close to each other.

In a matter of seconds danger and disaster had leaped in from the wings to occupy the stage.

The tugs, roughly abeam of each other and perhaps 100 feet apart, were being dragged irresistibly together with the 20,000 hulk astern sheering off to starboard at an acute angle. They were rapidly drawn together until only 15 or 20 feet separated them.

It was like a schoolmaster with his hands on the collars of two erring boys. By his thrust and swing he could bring them together until their heads would crack, except that in this case the two tugs would be dragged into collision with drama changing to tragedy in almost the twinkling of an eye.

There was but one thing to do and Captain Adam of *Bustler* did it. He ordered *Dexterous* to slip her tow. It had been previously arranged that in the event of any difficulty *Dexterous* would cast off, leaving the field of manœuvre to *Bustler*.

As the Chief Engineer of *Dexterous* was striking at the slip hook to release the tow the strain became too great and a large shackle parted. *Dexterous* was free, leaving *Bustler* to regain control of the errant *São Paulo*.

Up to then it had been little more than an accepted hazard of deep-sea towing and one with which both tug masters, and the head rigger on *São Paulo*, were familiar.

The picture as it no doubt presented itself was that *Bustler* would sternly bring the tow to heel, *Dexterous* would re-connect and the tow would proceed.

Then Fate, which always taps first, like a blacksmith measuring a piece of steel before aiming the heavy blow, struck hard.

São Paulo was still sheering off to starboard, and the strain was too great for *Bustler's* tow. It parted at *São Paulo's* end. The water-soaked heavy tow created unusual difficulty in heaving-in, remembering, of course, that all ships were being tossed about in a gale like corks on a turbulent stream. And then something happened which all towing men dread, whether it be a trawler towing a trawl, or a canal tug towing a barge, or a deep-sea tug with a hulk astern. The five-inch wire fouled *Bustler's* propeller, was parted and was lost.

That was about half-past five on a gale-riven evening, darkness setting in, the weather getting worse so that at times the wind rose to Force 12 on the Beaufort scale; in layman's language, it was a hurricane.

And somewhere in that gathering darkness was the hapless *São Paulo*.

Bustler's radar, with a range of 30 miles, started its search; her radio stabbed into the ether.

But all was silent. Neither radio nor radar could find her.

Through the tempestuous night the two tugs searched, red-rimmed eyes probing into a spume- and rain-lashed darkness in which every thickening of the blackness might have meant that they had found again the *São Paulo*.

It is seldom really opaque-dark ashore, but at sea, in bad weather the darkness can be as in the nethermost pit.

If you want to reconstruct it, put yourself in a really dark cellar where you cannot see your hand if it be held before your eyes. Get somebody to throw a bucket of water slap in your face at intervals of every half-minute. Imagine you are looking for the towering hulk of a ship charging about, wind and sea driven, in that darkness. You will be surprised how often you will fancy that the darkness thickens, takes on a degree of solidity. It was like that on the bridges of the *Bustler* and *Dexterous* that night of November 4th and the morning of November 5th.

The last they had seen of *São Paulo* was her dim red light receding into the darkness.

The problem facing Captain Adam and his colleague on *Dexterous* were: "How fast and how far is *São Paulo* drifting?" and "Is she still afloat?"

Had she still careered on, with a list, sheering off into the night, caught by the wind, her superstructure acting as sails on a sailing ship? Or had she swung round bow or stern on, and was she pitching and heaving close to them? Or had she gone down?

Through that night they searched and quartered the roaring sea, each moment expecting to see the hulk of *São Paulo* loom up, watching every moment to guard against ramming her in the darkness. And yet there was that nagging thought that, still in the grip of the wind, she was tearing away from them in an ever-increasing gap.

When the thought that she had been engulfed *did* occur they resolutely thrust it from them. In the general direction in which she was last seen, powerful signalling lamps occasionally flashed the signal: "We desire to communicate with you" —short, terse words in the Morse code.

But there was no answer.

Dexterous had no radar but *Bustler's* screen showed *Dexterous* about two and a half miles away, and for one brief period showed a blob which might have been *São Paulo*. The Court decided that in view of all the evidence that blob was "sea clutter", a confusion of close range echoes caused by the rearing seas close to.

A grey, wild morning showed no *São Paulo* and the search continued and widened. *Dexterous*, half the size of *Bustler*, was taking a heavy beating and in turning to begin another phase of the search she was swept by heavy seas and was so badly damaged that she had to limp to port.

Turmoil, away to the north, plunged to the scene and reached her by November 10th and she continued to search, quartering the sea extensively until November 20th. On November 19th *Bustler* had to leave for Lisbon to bunker-up again.

By this time any hope of finding *São Paulo* had diminished and the search was primarily to look for any survivors who might have got away in the *São Paulo's* ample life-saving gear.

In addition to the sister tugs, *Turmoil* and *Bustler*, aircraft of the Royal Air Force, United States Air Force and the

Portuguese Air Force covered thousands of miles in fruitless search.

There was only the vast, rolling sea, it having risen in its wrath, and claimed its victim.

Reluctantly on November 20th *Turmoil* turned north, giving up the search.

The findings of the Court were that both tugs were commanded by Masters of wide experience in salvage and towing. They were called before the Court and were assessed as being skilful navigators and reliable witnesses. In the Court's opinion, they handled their vessels and the tow with skill and diligence and with proper regard for safety.

Expert theories were produced in Court to try to explain the loss of the *São Paulo*, which, the Court considered, happened shortly after the tow parted. It was conjectured that the weight of the wind caused her to heel over until vulnerable gun ports were under water. She filled and a condition of foundering occurred.

Could a fanciful thought intrude here? Did perhaps the sea, in one of its rare merciful moments, say unto itself:

"Here is a ship which has been a gallant adversary for 40 years going to the ignominy of the breaker's yard. Such things cannot be. Come unto me ye that labour."

Better a last grim fight with the sea, and lose at sea, than the blinding, burning blowtorch.

A fanciful thought indeed, but did not the *Warspite*, another gallant fighter, flatly decline to be towed to the breakers, preferring the losing battle against the sea speared on the jagged rocks of Cornwall?

The epic of the *São Paulo* shows that deep-sea towing is not without its hazards, demands an extremely high standard of skill and unceasing watch and guard against the sea and all it can do.

CHAPTER THIRTEEN

WHICH can be the harder? A tow or a rescue job?

Any rescue tug Master will wrinkle his nose at that question and will give a reply akin to the flexible query: "How long is a piece of string?"

Some of Smit's tugs have towed vessels for thousands of miles and the entire voyage has been without any incident at all.

Yet a rescue attempt involving only a few miles' actual sea work has been packed hard with incident.

On the obverse, a rescue has been without incident and a tow full of problems as with the *São Paulo*.

No stage director would dare to arrange his settings with such sombre lighting and with such grim surrounds for even *Macbeth* or *Hamlet* as those which exist in real life round that grim stretch of coast which includes the western islands of Scotland, the Pentland Firth, the Orkneys and the Shetlands.

He would be accused of stretching life beyond any normal conception.

But those are the scenes for much of the work done by the tugs of Metal Industries (Salvage), Ltd., of which a typical example is *Salveda*.

Salveda is commanded by Herbert Sutherland, a man who has spent rather more than thirty years of his fifty in salvage and rescue work.

His ship *Salveda* "lives" at Kirkwall, that bleak little port in the north-east corner of the Orkneys, the place where, it is reputed, only one tree grows through the undying attention of the inhabitants and an absence of dogs.

Take a fairly large scale map of the north of Scotland, including the Orkneys and the Shetlands, and you have the stage on which *Salveda* plays out most of her drama.

There is a nice contrast between Captain Parker of *Turmoil* and Captain Sutherland of *Salveda*.

One is a man who came into rescue and salvage work almost by accident in the latter years of his life. The other is a man who has grown up in it from his stripling years and has known no other.

Yet both have that one quality—a sort of fierce dedication to the work they do, and both are seamen possessed of high qualities.

Parker works with the precision of a surgeon who, having made his diagnosis, proceeds fearlessly with the operation.

Sutherland, on the other hand, follows an instinct which must go many generations deep.

One example will serve, but to appreciate fully the point one would have to know the treacherous narrow, tide-ripped Western Isles.

One night Sutherland received a call by radio telephone to take *Salveda* through a strong westerly gale down to a ship which was in trouble in the Firth of Clyde.

There was a reasonably safe course outside the islands— the sea route—but Sutherland was bent on saving time.

He tackled the Corryvechan, a perilous trip in even calm weather in daytime, beset as it is with a tide race which can toss a ship about like a cork.

Sutherland put *Salveda* through it in the dark of a night without turning a hair and saved twelve precious hours, saved a merchant ship from twelve hours more of battering—and got her off.

Had he failed, of course, and put *Salveda* on any of the vicious rocks which waited . . .

There was the seaman drawing on his instinct. *Salveda* is 781 tons, 1,200 horsepower, built twelve years ago and is equipped with almost every form of salvage and towing gear imaginable. In addition to her sets of towing gear she has air compressors, pumps, oxy-electric and oxy-hydrogen under-

Casualty nicely tucked astern over the broad towing deck

Turmoil tows French troopship to Marseilles

Daylight showed the riven stern half of *World Concord*, a plunging, lethal wreck

Forty-eight hours later, safe in Holy Loch

water cutting gear, carries submarine blasting gelatine, and complete fire-fighting equipment including foam.

She sits at Kirkwall, waiting and watching, and her bill for a week for fuel, food and wages comes to around £500.

There is rivalry, of course, of the keenest order.

Parker recalls, with a sudden twinkle in his eyes, the occasion when he left his station and steamed *Turmoil* into the Bristol Channel because one of Metal Industries tugs was in difficulty with a tow. The tow had parted and the tail end of a wicked gale was playing ducks and drakes with tug and towed vessels.

Parker, then new to *Turmoil*, with suave politeness asked if he could try to put a tow aboard—and received a reluctant "yes", prompted probably by the fact that the towing tug thought it an impossibility. And it wasn't. The tow was put aboard, and although the towed hulk was intended for a Bristol Channel port the weather was such that Parker decided his best move was to run her up the Irish Sea. Which he did, with the original towing tug keeping close station.

That was Parker's triumph.

Any bookmaker would offer considerable odds that his eyes did not twinkle on another occasion, and would extend odds that they were considerably frosted.

On that occasion *Bustler, Turmoil's* sister ship, was under the Metal Industries house flag.

She, *Turmoil* and a Dutch ship, one of Smit's, the *Roode Zee*, were all lying at Falmouth, rolling easily to the light swell which was coming into the harbour, a residue of the half-gale outside.

A fruit-carrying ship lost her propeller a couple of hundred miles out in the Atlantic.

Turmoil, Bustler and *Roode Zee* started heaving anchor together with a uniformity which would have pleased any admiral.

Bustler had a slight contretemps with her anchor but the race was on.

K

Bustler reached the ship first and passed a tow. *Turmoil*, a few minutes astern, presumably had received radio instructions that his firm had been given the order by the ship's owners, and wanted to take over the tow.

Bustler's captain blandly questioned this and tightened on the tow a little so that it could not be slipped.

So in that order they proceeded to harbour, *Bustler* towing, *Turmoil* fuming and the *Roode Zee* watchful, so that if the tow parted she would be nearby to pass another.

Honours were even.

One feels that Hollywood would make a breath-taking scenario with that as a foundation.

There is rivalry, a keen and merciless rivalry, between these international rescue tug Masters and any one of them would without hesitation take the utmost of any fair advantage which came their way—and when they met afterwards over a humble gin on each other's ships would discuss it without rancour, even with a chuckle.

The Dutch and French ships know roughly where *Turmoil* is on station, and the *Turmoil* knows where they are. None of them knows when any one of the others may have left on a prosaic tow. But one wonders.

Over a period of years each tug company has built up a long and reliable series of contacts on every stretch of coast.

Frequently the midnight oil—in the form of modern electric light—burns in Overseas Towage & Salvage head-quarters in Houndsditch, London, in Smit's offices in West-plein, Rotterdam and at Metal Industries' headquarters overlooking Gare Loch, at Shandon, Dumbartonshire.

At Shandon, Mr. Murray Taylor, Metal Industries' chief salvage officer, and Mr. James Lightbody, the commercial manager, are available for twenty-four hours in every day.

Sutherland and *Salveda*, of course, often work in waters which would appal even seasoned deep-sea rescue tug Masters.

Much of his "beat" is around the treacherous Western

Isles, the forbidding Orkneys and Shetlands and that fearsome
stretch of water, the Pentland Firth, where the tide sometimes
runs at nine lethal knots.

One example will serve.

Early in spring the Swedish tanker *Oljaren* went ashore at
Muckle Skerry in the Pentland Firth.

At its most vicious the Pentland Firth can daunt even the
bravest heart. Men who know the waters, with their whirl-
pools and overfalls, claim that no ship, once firmly aground
there, can be rescued.

Oljaren, with a cargo worth nearly a million pounds, was
well and truly ashore. The crash had torn open her bottom and
after one look a Dutch tug decided that there was just another
victim for the Pentlands.

Sutherland took one of those gambles—drawing on his
instinct—which lends support to a claim made by those who
know him that often he is mystic, or, as the Scots say, is
"fey".

He decided that if he could lighten her and fill part of her
with compressed air she might be refloated. There was nothing
outrageous in that assessment. It was almost a normal approach
up to then, and a job which was frequently done, but Sutherland was gambling on the unpredictable weather of that area.
So unpredictable in fact that from a chill but sunny afternoon
it can progress to a dark and howling gale in a matter of
minutes.

She was lightened; a salvage party worked for nearly three
weeks replacing heavy diesel oil in the tanks with compressed
air.

By the end of April she was ready to float—and the weather
struck.

The air-packed *Oljaren*, buoyant and ready to float off,
began to pound heavily.

Sutherland nursed *Salveda* through terrific seas to pass a
towline—without success. It looked as if the work of three
weeks would end—as so many rescue attempts had ended in

those waters—in debris marking the spot where once was a ship.

Sutherland backed *Salveda* away, stood alone on the bridge, introspective, silent, and his crew wondered if he was admitting defeat.

Then suddenly he said: "We'll try again in fifteen minutes."

What difference a quarter of an hour would make nobody on board *Salveda* but Sutherland could assess.

In fifteen minutes he crept *Salveda* in, stern first, with perfect timing. "Like a woman edging a pram in through a shop doorway," as one of the crew afterwards described it. In . . . closer . . . her stern lifting and falling in the heavy seas until the tow was passed from hand to hand.

Oljaren was towed off, the sea reluctantly gave up the battle, the wind eased. Weather-wise members of the crew say that there was no indication, when Sutherland moved in, that the wind was going to ease. Did he draw on some extra instinct that men of the Orkneys have and develop?

Men who served in the Navy at Scapa say one does develop an extra sea sense. Sutherland seems to have it highly developed.

The award for salvage of the *Oljaren*, based on value of the ship and cargo, was £750,000. All of which might have been lost but for one man following his instinct.

Salveda, like all other rescue and salvage tugs, works on the "no cure, no pay" basis and on that foundation a mistake can be costly, and success profitable.

Often three tugs will race for a ship in distress knowing that the first tug there to offer a tow on the Lloyds' standard form of "no cure, no pay" will get the job, and the others will have had their slam through the gale for nothing.

It is part of the game.

When the Costa Rican motor-ship *Sousy* ran into trouble off the Cornish coast late in 1954 Tim Bond, in his tug *Englishman*, was at Falmouth. Parker in *Turmoil* was on his station at Cobh. Both sailed to assist.

The weather got progressively worse as they slammed into the gale. Bond had to round the Lizard and Land's End and steam into the entrance of the Bristol Channel; Parker had to slam across the Irish Sea.

In the meantime, the *Sousy*, with two of her crew injured, was heading helplessly for that graveyard of ships—a hundred miles of coast without a sheltering port—the north Cornwall and Devon coast.

Standing by the *Sousy* was the British destroyer *Savage*. She had been on passage from Scotland to Devonport when she picked up *Sousy's* call for help.

Savage searched for her, found her and succeeded in passing a tow. No mean feat for a destroyer. That tow parted and the crippled ship was not more than 10 miles from St. Ives—a delectable spot for a holiday, but no place on which a crippled ship should drift.

After twelve hours Tim Bond reached the *Sousy* first and got his tow aboard on a "no cure, no pay" agreement.

Turmoil could do no more than stand by, writing off the expense of her journey into a vicious sea.

The "no cure, no pay" agreement is worth a little explanation.

Lloyds have drawn up a standard form of offer which all rescue tug Masters carry, and in fact keep a few signed by themselves ready in their berths.

As they close a crippled ship they either offer a tow by radio or by signal, asking the captain if he agrees to accept a tow on that standard form of agreement.

He knows the terms and accepts; the tow is passed and the crippled ship is taken to port.

What payment follows does not concern the tug Master.

His owners and the owners of the ship accept arbitration on the amount of the award.

Just plain business.

Sometimes a shipowner, learning that his ship is in trouble, will contact the tug owners and arrange a tow direct with them.

That should, and invariably does, mean that the tug has the job; the captain of the ship has been advised and waits to pass his tow.

There are slips; a ship is not advised in time, or, as in the case of *Bustler* and the fruit liner, the first ship in passes a tow and then spends time arguing—and towing.

Ultimately these differences are settled in E.C. 3—and become topics for bantering conversation when tug Masters meet.

There was the not unamusing situation when *Turmoil*, working on orders from her owners, proceeded to the rescue of the Norwegian ship *Mildred* which was on fire in the North Sea. Her orders were flexible: take her in tow, extinguish fire if possible and either take the ship into Harwich or beach her as conditions imposed.

Parker at this time was on leave and a temporary captain was in command of *Turmoil*.

Turmoil closed the ship, edging alongside, watching the rolling smoke coming from her, and to her skipper's surprise he found a small French trawler, less than quarter the size of *Turmoil*, fast to the ship's stern.

He put a small party aboard and they found a little group of French fishermen complete with French tricolour which they had hoisted. It signified nothing, of course, as *Turmoil* was on a contract to take the ship in tow.

But not to *Turmoil's* tough crew.

"Give us a red ensign. We'll hoist that too."

Her captain entered into the spirit of things and sent a boat ensign over, so there was the amusing spectacle of *Turmoil* fast to one end of the burning ship, her towing-party standing under a red ensign, and at the other end of the ship was the French trawler, also fast, and her party under the French tricolour.

Possibly the trawler skipper, with but a hazy knowledge of the complex laws of salvage, felt that as long as he had a party and a flag aboard he would be entitled to some of the trimmings.

A brave thought, and there are no Court of Arbitration findings available to show whether his superb optimism was tangibly supported.

Turmoil, of course, with her powerful engines towed the burning ship plus the French trawler, which was futilely trying to steam the other way. Her effort had little effect except to cause *Turmoil's* captain to increase his engine revolutions. Even with the trawler engines going full speed *Turmoil* was quite capable of pulling the trawler and ship all over the North Sea.

"It was like trying to wheel a barrow with a frisky dog tied to it on a longish lead," one of *Turmoil's* crew said.

The French towing-party and the British towing-party obeyed a hastily improvised protocol. The Frenchmen stayed on their part of the ship and the *Turmoil's* party on the other, with the billowing smoke as the frontier between them.

Amused glances pass between members of *Turmoil's* crew when they relate that the Frenchmen, with eyes reddened and swollen, did once clamber beyond the smoke curtain, and ordered the *Turmoil's* party to pull down the red ensign.

"We said 'No'—and the ensign stayed put," one of *Turmoil's* petty officers relates.

One diffidently feels that in the post mortem account the dialogue has become seriously abbreviated and has departed from the original script, an opinion strengthened by having seen *Turmoil's* crew lined up against a bar, and having listened to their virile conversation.

But, for the record, they declined and the ensign remained. So be it.

The same petty officer glossed over the fact that for a few minutes *Turmoil's* boarding party were in real danger of losing their lives when they first climbed on board *Mildred*.

So far as they could see the fire was roughly amidships. Smoke was pouring from every hole there, the deck was red hot and threatening to burst open like a blossoming flower at any moment.

Armed with heavy extinguishers and dragging foam pipes after them they crept as close to the fire as they could and started their fight.

Suddenly behind them there was a deafening roar. They turned to find that the fire had broken out between them and the end of the ship. They were trapped. No longer could they battle with the flames amidships. They had to concentrate on subduing the new outbreak sufficiently to create a small opening through which they could retreat.

Three times they beat the flames down, three times the flames regained a hold. Finally, at the fourth attempt, they smothered the flames sufficiently to momentarily make a slim gap and they got through—with empty extinguishers and the foam hoses perishing in the fire.

The original fire and the new outbreak joined forces to present a larger problem, a problem eventually solved by "Bill" Carnegy, one of *Turmoil's* engineers. Lying on a float, sometimes almost entirely submerged, he cut a hole in her side with a blow torch, a hole below the waterline so that the sea could rush in and put out the fire.

Finally, with *Mildred* resting on the bottom in shallow water, and the fire out, he did the same task in reverse. Half under water he put a patch over the hole and helped to instal powerful pumps to eject the water he had let in.

"Bill" Carnegy, by the way, has literally grown up in salvage and towing.

His father worked for Metal Industries at Scapa Flow taking "Bill" with him when *Turmoil's* engineer was a few weeks old. The shore plant and the tugs were his playground. As he grew up the tugs became his world. He has sailed in Metal Industries tugs, among them *Bustler* when she was under their flag.

A tug man to the core with a fund of tug stories.

Rescue and towing tug Masters treat their operations with a cold approach. To them a ship being towed has no personality. It is briefly "the tow" and a ship in trouble is "the casualty" until she is fast to the tug and is being taken to harbour. Then she, too, becomes "the tow".

But there some rare moments in their lives when they allow a little glow of warmth to enter into their work.

Parker of *Turmoil* has one. To him his attempt to tow *Flying Enterprise* to harbour was just a job, and in his estimate would not have been too difficult but for various factors such as shortage of crew on board the freighter, his late start, the contrary, vicious weather, and the fact that her hatches burst open.

A moment he likes to remember with warmth, a warmth which lights up his eyes even when he discusses it three or four years afterwards, was the moment he moved in resolutely to the sinking *Flying Enterprise* to take Dancy and Carlsen off the horizontal smokestack.

He saw them jump, watched their heads in the water—then they were on board, weary, dripping wet and defeated.

"When I shook hands with him I felt I was shaking hands with a REAL man," Parker says. "And my admiration has not diminished over the years. I admire him intensely."

Another such moment must have come to Sutherland of *Salveda*. At the time he was in command of *Metinda II*.

Metal Industries have several tugs with names coined from syllables of "Metal Industries", e.g. *Metinda I*, *Metinda II*, *Metinda III*, etc.

Shortly after the war, *Salveda*, which later was to become Sutherland's command, ran on the rocks.

Metinda II was sent to salvage her. It was a ticklish job with complete failure no great distance away.

And Sutherland got her off.

Does it require much imagination to feel what he felt when later he was given command of her and climbed up to her bridge? One can almost hear him whisper, "Well, we meet again."

CHAPTER FOURTEEN

A QUEEN of England is reputed to have once said: "After I am dead you will find 'Calais' written upon my heart."

Subsequent history does not tell us whether any post mortem surgical research found anything untoward with the good lady's cardiac organ.

But if there is some celestial engraver who does imprint a record of major events on people's hearts, then somewhere on the heart of Captain Daniel Parker of *Turmoil* would be found the words *World Concord*.

He rescued one half of this ship, which broke in two in the Irish Sea in November, 1954, and fought hellish weather over more than 300 miles before he finally got her into the Clyde.

Tug Masters, who are the supreme judges of the tactics and methods used by a rival, are not prone to be lavish in their praise but they agree that Parker's efforts, and the work of his crew, on that rescue bid were superb.

It was a rescue with all the cards stacked against the tug.

Then came, a couple of months later, a purely commercial tow, to take the same half of the tanker to Antwerp from Belfast.

And again the weather waited in ambush, and all Parker's skill and the power of *Turmoil* were called upon to prevent that tow from ending in disaster.

It started late in November. *Turmoil* was waiting and ready at her station. There were gale warnings in operation from Rockall, Hebrides, Irish Sea, Fastnet, Biscay, Bristol Channel, Plymouth and Dover.

In short, the Atlantic unleashing itself in a November gale, merciless, destructive.

Parker slipped from his quay and went out to sea late at night in answer to a call of distress from a small coaster which had been caught out in bad weather and was in difficulties. Scarcely had *Turmoil* cleared the sheltered roads and met the full fury of the gale when the small ship radioed that she was no longer in need of assistance.

Parker knew his eastern Atlantic when it is in a savage mood and on a hunch decided to stay at sea, just jogging along easily, not fighting the gale.

Then, early in the morning, he received a signal that the tanker *World Concord*, of 20,000 tons, had broken into halves at the southern end of the Irish Sea.

Turmoil's easy jog became a rolling race.

As she slugged away further signals told him that the aircraft carrier *H.M.S. Indefatigable* and the sloop *H.M.S. Orwell* were standing by the fore part, which still had some of the crew aboard.

Signals were rather confused—not surprising! The sea was lashed into a fury, the wind was whipping the tops off the waves and turning them into blinding showers of stinging spray. Added to that were squalls of rain which reduced visibility to less than the length of the tug.

Let us look at the construction of a conventional tanker to understand the problem fully.

A tanker is, as the name implies, a vast tank. Her engines and main accommodation are all at the after part of the ship. Half way along, with large tank space between, is the bridge, then more tank space and finally the bow.

World Concord, in ballast (that is, unladen), had broken in two so that the engines and part of the deck were in one part, and the bridge and fore part of the ship constituted the other.

When she broke the watch on deck, seven men, officers and a few seamen, were on the bridge; the remainder of the crew were on the after part.

Captain Athanassiou, who commanded the *World Concord*, afterwards described the moment of breaking.

"We had left Liverpool in ballast for the Middle East and had reached the south end of the Irish Sea. About two o'clock in the morning the ship suddenly broke in two. It was quite noiseless, and there was no warning. Afterwards both parts met again in a crashing collision."

Again there is that spectacle. The sea, waiting and watching, hammering and probing, seeking to find that error of omission or commission, or both, so that it can demand its victim and overwhelm it. Striking in full fury in the early morning—that hour when man's resistance is at its lowest.

After smashing together the two parts drifted away into the night. The fore part, with the seven men aboard, was down heavily in the water at one end with the other cocked up high in the air. The after part remained on a fairly even keel.

That was the situation when *Turmoil* rounded the heel of Ireland. Somewhere in that cockpit between the Welsh and Irish coast were the two halves of the 20,000 tons tanker.

Parker was told then that the after part had gone down and he concentrated on the fore part. He followed his usual practice and edged *Turmoil* in close to the bow of the tanker and passed a tow. That was made fast, but the sea was not willing to give up its victim without a fight of much sterner quality.

A wave larger and more powerful than the others which had been battering the two ships came roaring up out of the darkness. The tug and part of the ship surged inwards towards each other like two gyrating dancers, bobbed together, then swung apart.

No tow made by man could stand it and there came the disheartening cry, "Tow's pa-a-a-rted!"

Parker studied his casualty. She was racing along like a full-rigged ship, riding the seas with a degree of confidence and was going right up the middle of the Channel. With reasonable luck, and with daylight only a few hours away, he could afford to keep close station on her ready for an emergency—and wait. So he did.

In the meantime, the other half, the stern part of the ship, had not sunk as had been reported but had drifted diagonally towards the Welsh coast. The thirty-five men on it were rescued by St. David's lifeboat and were landed safely.

Parker was manœuvring *Turmoil* to put another tow aboard the fore part when the Rosslare lifeboat came out, manned by those redoubtable Irish characters who make living history of their rescues.

Then came the news that the after part was in danger of going ashore somewhere off Bardsey Island, in Cardigan Bay. Once ashore, with the battering sea hammering it, that part of the casualty would soon become a total wreck.

Parker signalled to the captain of the tanker—or at least to the part commanded by the captain—telling him of his assessment of the situation. The fore part was in no immediate danger whereas the after part could become a total wreck. Parker proposed to tear off after the drifting half which was threatening to go ashore, intending to rescue that and come back for the remainder.

And that he did.

Acting on information received, as the police say, *Turmoil* searched for and found the stern half. It had missed Bardsey Island but was in danger of going ashore on the Welsh coast north of that and had followed a diagonal course from the Irish southern coast to the northern Welsh coast, whereas the front part was going right up the middle of the Channel.

"What amazed me at the time, and still amazes me, was the speed over the ground these two halves made," Parker says. "They went along like full-rigged ships homeward bound with a fair wind and a tide to catch."

The stern half of course had no crew aboard, they having been landed by the lifeboat from St. David's.

So the problem was to get a tow aboard.

Parker sent away his powerful motor boat with a crew of four and a volunteer party of five, headed by Mr. Davies, the Second Mate.

There, in twenty-five words, is an epic.

A gale was still lashing the sea into young mountains, and

to take nine men from his total crew of twenty-seven left Parker extremely short-handed on his tug. But there was no other way.

The volunteer crew in charge of Mr. Davies included the Chief Steward, a radio operator for communication purposes, and two seamen.

There is no closed shop on rescue tugs, at least not on *Turmoil*. When Parker calls for volunteers from his crew the first five forward win—and the remainder retire disgruntled, determined to quicken up their reflexes on the next occasion.

The motor boat returned and was shipped and the passing of the tow took place. Yet another minor epic described in fifteen words, but passed it was.

The stern half, a clumsy squared hull, without the clean entry of the bow portion, a mass of debris hanging from it, with the rudder and screws to affect steering, was no easy tow to contemplate, but it was in tow.

The wind was still westerly; vicious, but it had eased slightly compared to the screaming gale of the last thirty hours or so.

Parker started his long haul over from the Welsh coast towards the Irish coast which would give him some sort of lee, a measure of shelter.

His tow was sheering about, at times coming up almost to his beam, then slamming across to the other side.

Then from the Admiralty *Turmoil* received a signal which sent cold shivers down Parker's spine.

His tow was part of a vessel, a tanker, which had not been degassed before sailing. In other words, the tanks were probably —in fact, were—full of an unstable, volatile explosive gas capable of ripping the half ship into smithereens.

And from a hundred gaps in that riven hull the gas was seeping.

No signal ever passed so quickly from one ship to another as *Turmoil* signalled to the heroic little party on board the half-hull, telling them not to smoke on any account.

There was another danger. There were riven plates grinding

one another as the hull rose and fell in the heavy sea. One spark from two pieces of metal meeting would be enough to turn the hull into a vast, rose-red blossom of flame framed in billowing, thick black smoke. Even the tow, grinding and whipping, could produce the fatal spark.

The hours crept by as *Turmoil* moved towards Belfast Lough, the hands of the clock dragging.

But the weather had not finished.

Turmoil reached close in to the Irish coast between the inlet Carlingford and Belfast Lough, sheltered waters.

And the wind swung round to the east, came raving over the Irish Sea, catching *Turmoil*, with her unwieldy tow, only a few miles from a lee shore. The problem then became not one of progress forward but of battling for precious distance outwards, away from the coast.

To enter Belfast Lough with the wind in that direction would have been suicidal. Parker decided that he would make for the Clyde.

Now, once again, study a map of that area from Belfast Lough northwards. There is the bottleneck of the North Channel plentifully sprinkled with what the cartographer has described as overfalls, tide rips and strong tides.

North of the North Channel opens the Clyde. Look at it. It stands like a spread of talons. There is the long, stabbing finger of Galloway, rock-bound and merciless, then the Mull of Kintyre and north and west of that the Island of Islay. And right in the middle is Arran and Bute with the rock sentinel of Ailsa Craig to cramp any movement.

Nowhere is there more than a few miles in which to fight desperately for a little elbow room.

For anybody daunted at the prospect of tackling the Clyde and deciding to keep clear, Rathlin Island waits grimly to take its quota.

But the wind was easterly and that spread of hand of Galloway and Kintyre meant a nice protecting weather coast for *Turmoil* and her tow. The wind reached howling force again as *Turmoil* battled towards the Clyde, often with tug and tow pointing dead into the wind and progressing sideways like vehicles in a long skid. But it was progress, with the protecting shore looming up ever nearer.

Once *Turmoil* was within the grasp of that vast rock hand, with Galloway on her starboard beam, the wind dropped.

Weather-wise, Parker waited, knowing what was coming, and worked his tow round to meet it. It came.

The wind swung round to the west and screamed down in triumph.

It now became a battle to get what seamen call an "offing", room to work away from the protecting coast, which in a short interval had become a menace.

Turmoil battled towards the north-west, straining away at the load behind her, battling to get north and west of Ailsa Craig.

After hours and hours of ceaseless battle, a short distance on the chart, Ailsa Craig crept slowly astern.

Rather more than half this battle had taken place in darkness, with only approximate bearing on lights which were as often as not shrouded in lashing, obscuring rain.

It was a pale wind-swept dawn which found *Turmoil* edging nearer to safety.

Finally, declining help from smaller tugs, *Turmoil* berthed her half of the tanker in Holy Loch and the weary tow party returned on board—longing for a smoke.

Captain Parker is not given to dealing out lavish praise. His crew is on board to do a job of work—work which often involves taking a risk.

On this occasion he thawed.

"They were heroes, every one of them. I wouldn't like to single out any man, either from the crew which took over the motor boat and put the volunteers aboard or from the men who climbed aboard her. Huge waves buffeted them as they went aboard and I was glad when that part was over. When I received the signal that she had not been degassed I was worried until it was sent over to the half astern. They were sitting on dynamite. You know what happens when you throw a match into an empty petrol tin? Well, that would have happened a million times greater. Knowing that a spark would do it, even from a bit of steel plating jarring, the crew on the half tanker went over her, surveying her every watch and reported back to me."

One wishes that the facts could be endorsed on their discharge books, those laconic reports on a seaman's character.

The other part of the tanker, after her seven men had been taken off by Rosslare lifeboat, swept more or less serenely up the Irish Sea and was taken in tow by the tug *Cautious*.

That was Parker and *Turmoil's* part in the rescue of the split tanker *World Concord*.

The halves were patched up, were taken to Belfast in readiness for removal to a dockyard which would join them together again.

And one day in February Parker received a signal.

It was to proceed to Belfast to take in tow for Antwerp the stern half of the *World Concord*.

The bow half, also at Belfast, would be towed by *Salveda* and another tug.

Turmoil's crew said: "This was where we came in."

But this was no hair-raising dash after a gas-filled derelict. This was merely a tow, a bread-and-butter task.

But was it?

L

CHAPTER FIFTEEN

Turmoil reached Belfast Lough on a day of almost flat calm, a chill, yellow-tinged day, bitterly cold, with the sky filled with specks of green and brass, and the sea had an ominous leaden tint about it.

There, waiting for her, was her erstwhile "casualty", now to become her "tow".

The ragged, jagged edges of the break had been more or less trimmed, the gaping holes had been shored up and she was watertight. She promised to be an awkward tow; she would have to be taken stern first with the squared-off, patched-up break dragging through the water pulling nearly her own weight in water behind it.

The forepart, with *Salveda* in charge, had already set sail and was perhaps better equipped to meet any emergencies because it had the anchors and cables.

Furthermore, it had the clean, sharp bow to enter the water and make the tow a little less irksome.

The stern half was equipped with an anchor and cable of sorts but which would be of little use except for holding her in sheltered waters in reasonable weather.

Turmoil set off veering 350 fathoms of tow made fast to the stern of the half-tanker. That is, rather more than 2,000 feet of tow out.

Scarcely had the tug and its tow cleared Belfast Lough when the wind leaped savagely from ambush.

The towing log records briefly: "Wind S.W., force 7/8."

A gale in any language.

It whipped up a vicious short, steep sea and more powerful gusts took charge of the unwieldy tow and sent it sheering wildly from one side to another.

Soon Parker realized that *Turmoil*, far from making headway, or even holding her own against the south-west gale, was sagging off towards the ragged coast which waited only a few miles to the east.

He was back in the arena where he had fought the elements for the same victim less than three short months before.

To the north and east of him waited the same clutching talons, the Mull of Galloway, the Mull of Kintyre, with Arran, Rathlin and Islay there in the way so that if he evaded one he would fall foul of another.

Once again he attempted to turn tug and tow head to wind but the battering elements, the sea and the wind, were bent on defeating that manœuvre this time.

He did get *Turmoil* facing the Irish coast and inching in towards the shelter it could offer. Tug and tow were broadside on to the wind and sea and going rapidly north-east, whereas his course should have been south.

Darkness found him in approximately the same position as he had been on another memorable dark night a few weeks back. And again it became guesswork, with succeeding fixes being only approximate.

Through the darkness she plunged, out on one quarter was the clumsy tow, fortunately this time degassed and without any of *Turmoil's* crew aboard. The tow sagged deeply in the water. Then suddenly the half tanker would come charging furiously through the night, would loom up out of the darkness, white waves cresting up over her. She would sheer off to the other quarter and the tow wire would twang bar-tight.

He was getting some shelter from the Irish coast and went in closer until he was only two miles or so away. He intended waiting until the weather eased, if only comparatively briefly, so that he could move down into the wider waters of the Irish Channel where he would have more elbow-room.

It was as if the weather, profiting by its previous defeat, had waited for him to get into just that position.

With scarcely any warning it backed and came from the south-east with even greater force.

L*

With the same derelict in tow, in the same place, at the same time in the early hours of the morning, the same thing had happened. *Turmoil* was almost within sight of the dreaded white water as the waves lashed over the rocks inshore.

Once again *Turmoil* had to wear around, to battle from that coast and head over towards the Scottish coast. Through the night, sometimes with the half-hull abeam of her on one side, then surging away to abeam on the other, *Turmoil* struggled along.

Once the tow line, sagging deeply after one of the hull's wide surges, caught in an obstruction on the bottom, but hauled clear.

Again there was that heart-breaking slug over towards the Scottish coast somewhere in the darkness ahead—how far was guesswork.

From Port Patrick *Turmoil* got a fix which showed that she was close to the Scottish coast, and in fact the shelter was becoming obvious. Through that narrow bottleneck the half of *World Concord* and *Turmoil* wearily plunged, often both heading dead east while their course over the ground was almost north.

In the dark hours before dawn she hauled up past the long arm of the Mull of Galloway and before her yawned the gap between the Mull of Kintyre and Galloway, with the Clyde opening up behind.

Still the wind remained south-easterly, still vicious but partly disarmed by the shelter from the land.

Then the wind went for its knockout. As *Turmoil* and the tow crept past the top knuckle of Galloway the wind shrieked down through a loch, swinging tug and tow until they were beam-on—and swiftly changed back to south-west again at even greater force.

Turmoil and the half-tanker were once again caught on a lee shore, with no room to work, and to windward Ailsa Craig stabbing upwards in the middle, with Arran and Kintyre offering a jagged, ship-breaking finish.

There was no time for niceties, or delicacy of touch. *Turmoil* and tow had to go hell-for-leather to get away from that rocky coast immediately above the Mull of Galloway and to prevent the little cavalcade from being blown and hammered over towards Kintyre or Arran.

For long hours the stout tow was often bar-tight and twanging with a deep-toned boom which at any moment could end with a loud crack.

At one time the hull of the tanker was out at right angles to *Turmoil* with the tow line ninety degrees from the line of *Turmoil's* tow deck.

Despite concealing paint, she still has the scars on her deck-house aft where the wire chafed and thudded.

By daylight Parker knew that he had won that round, at least. This time he had passed south of Ailsa Craig and had reached sheltered waters from whichever quarter the wind chose to come.

And the wind gave up the battle. It died away, leaving the stage dimly lit with the same green-brass tinge as on the hour when *Turmoil* sailed from Belfast Loch.

Finally, after rather more favourable weather forecasts, *Turmoil* set sail once more to follow *Salveda* and her consort, which, having reached the broader waters of the Irish Sea, had battled downwards towards Land's End.

The weather was no more than boisterous on the trip down but snarled a threat as they rounded Land's End and the Lizard.

There were problems, involving the inadequacy of the anchoring equipment, which perturbed Parker, knowing as he did that he would be getting into close waters and might have to anchor.

He took the lead from *Salveda* and her tow—although it was by no means a race—and eventually, passing the Goodwins, he headed up towards the mouth of the Scheldt.

That stretch of coast is perhaps better known to holiday-makers from this country than is the Clyde and Irish Sea.

It can be charming in its season and deadly when it is bad weather.

There are sandbanks galore, the depth of water shallows allowing comparatively little wind to pile up a short and punishing sea. Furthermore, sometimes hidden beneath the surface but at others just showing, are wrecks innumerable, melancholy memorials to man-made war and the merciless sea.

It was as if the wind and sea, balked of their prey farther west, called themselves into council, saying: "Let us have one more try. We have got this tug and her tow into narrow, restricted waters. If we hit her with our combined full force there is nothing they can do. They cannot go on up the Scheldt at night time. Small tugs will not, or cannot, come out to take her over. She is ours. So—into battle!"

And into battle it was. Farther west small ships were sunk by that gale; higher up the east coast of Holland and Denmark other ships ran into trouble and some were lost. And that gale, in darkness, *Turmoil* had once more to fight.

After an exchange of messages Parker received permission to enter Flushing.

Like all northern Continental ports, Flushing's opening lies across-tide, and in this case nearly across-wind. It was an operation offering a wealth of trouble, even disaster, for the slightest miscalculation. She had to shorten in tow and sidle up against wind and tide with the narrow opening of Flushing almost at right angles.

Two small tugs came out to help in the last stages and gradually Parker edged closer in towards the port.

At the right moment he turned on full power, swung his bow round, bringing the half-tanker to follow obediently. And *Turmoil* and *World Concord*—or half of it—had reached safety.

Once more, almost incredibly, the wind died away in a moan of defeat. *Turmoil* had won.

The following day the half of *World Concord* was taken on

up the Scheldt to await the fore part, which was still labouring along and ultimately arrived twelve days afterwards.

Turmoil's first contact with the stern half of *World Concord* was a salvage job. Parker towed it—nay, fought the elements for it—for nearly fifty hours and steamed approximately 300 miles from the time he put his tow party aboard until he took her into Holy Loch. And that was an epic condensed into just over two days.

His next contact, when he took her over as a tow, from the first time he made fast at Belfast Lough until he finally handed her over in the Scheldt, was nearly two weeks and he steamed again—the term is *fought* for her—over rather more than a thousand miles.

There is only one description for that, also. It was an epic.

World Concord, possibly by the time this book appears, will be joined together again and will once more steam the wide oceans.

It might be that hastening along on her lawful occasions she might meet *Turmoil*—on a slow and prosaic tow.

And the sea, admitting defeat—if only for the time being—will wryly get under their bows and lift them upwards in a curtsey of acknowledgment, *World Concord* to whisper, in the way ships do whisper, a brief "Thanks!" and *Turmoil* to say: "That is what I'm here for, the reason for my being—that, and the tow behind me."

A wayward and fanciful thought, but without such thoughts the life at sea would be a dismal, empty existence.

CHAPTER SIXTEEN

Rescue tugs and their crews are not unlike the ambulance or fire-fighting men ashore. Much of their time is spent in the boredom of just waiting until a major or minor disaster calls for their participation. Then they go into action.

The crew is departmentalized in the same way as the crew of any other merchant ship. There is the deck department, officers and petty officers; there is the engine-room staff; there are stewards and cooks and the radio officers. There the similarity ends.

Men can sail on a merchant ship as either deck officers and engineer officers for a couple of years and never reach any real familiarity, and the same state of affairs exists to a certain extent with the crews.

It goes back to the days when steam first invaded the holy precincts of sail.

Deck officers are apt to claim that ships were sailed before steam was discovered as a means of propulsion. Engineers argue back that if they shut down their engines the ships would soon be just so much scrap-iron.

It is a fatuous argument, the fundamentals of which are lost in maritime antiquity but are still vaguely preserved in more or less acrimonious debate between engine-room and deck.

Somehow that argument ceases to hold water when men ship on rescue tugs.

There could be two reasons. On a merchant ship the two departments maintain what the law calls in cases of marital separation "independent establishments". The engineers have their quarters and their own mess-room, and steward and the deck officers have theirs. And seldom the twain meet, except to discuss a technical point.

But on the rescue tugs—it prevails on *Turmoil* and without

a doubt is the same the tug service throughout—all, from Master down to the youngest engineer, use the same dining-room, or what was in their naval days the wardroom.

It is when men forgather over a meal that barriers break down, even if other vehement arguments of a wider scope take their place.

During a meal time the Chief Officer, Mr. Lindsay, the Chief Engineer, Mr. E. Bell, and Captain Parker will be seated at one table and the talk will range from the iniquities of shore stevedores, based on Mr. Lindsay's experience, the financial blizzard which hit America in the 30's, as told by Mr. Bell, to a story of a cruise on a palatial yacht, owned by a millionaire, with a crew of seventy-five, from the tongue of Captain Parker.

At the other end of the room junior deck and engineer officers will be discussing the merits of a certain footballer and whether he is worth the price paid for his transfer, switching swiftly to the chances of a horse in a forthcoming big race, finally to round up on the charms of a fair Hebe in a favourite hostelry ashore.

Unconsciously the officers of both departments are de-molishing the barriers that exist between their departments on merchant ships and are getting together.

That could be one contributing factor, but the other, and possibly the more important one, is that when a rescue tug is on a job then there is no room for rigid caste barriers. First into the boat is first away. We have seen how a steward and a radio operator joined in the towage party which went aboard the *World Concord*. They have done it before; they will do it again. The man handling a heavy line in an emergency might easily have a boy steward tailing on behind him (and thoroughly enjoying his brief freedom from more humble duties).

They work as a team, each recognizing the virtues of the other and leaving any full-blooded revelations of shortcomings to subsequent light-hearted inquests when the first pints are on the bar.

There would be no room for any other form of life in a ship which has a crew of only 27, and moments for swift and strong action come, as they do come and will come again.

Things are not perfect—they never were—and while there may be grumbles and growls there is on the whole a fierce, possessive pride.

The gear they have to handle would frighten a person ashore.

Ranged round her towing deck are vast steel shackles weighing thirty pounds or more, each greased and ready for instant use, each capable of taking the strain of a towed ship of 20,000 tons or more.

Reeled up on her electric winch are hundreds of fathoms of five-inch wire rope. Down in the hold on the after deck, or coiled and lashed, are thousands of feet of wire rope ranging from three-inch to five-inch, and coils of manilla rope 20 inches or more in diameter, almost as thick as a girl's waist.

These towing ropes and wires more often than not have to be handled with the deck heaving and pitching and sea coming aboard in considerable quantities, and in darkness to complicate the hazard.

Rescue tug owners have not been slow to avail themselves of the sciences. In addition to four or five radio sets, they are equipped with radar and duplicate echo-sounding sets.

In another direction science has not been neglected.

One of the enemies of towing is weight of tow. Once it is in the water weight can be an advantage as the sag acts as a spring against any snatch, but handling it, and for a distressed ship's crew to get it aboard, water-soaked and heavy, can sometimes lead to defeat, or at least many hours of hard work, as we have seen with *Flying Enterprise*.

Most of the tugs are now equipped with nylon hawsers. Weight for size, the nylon is stronger than a manilla twice its thickness, does not become waterlogged and is considerably easier to handle.

For a long tow tug Masters endeavour to make their tow up

of manilla or nylon and wire in various parts so that there is a degree of resilience, and it takes an almighty powerful snatch to part a tow so made up.

A nylon tow of 500 fathoms can cost as much as £3,000. And wire and manilla are quite expensive, so nobody is careless with gear costing that amount of money.

There is a wealth of other gear; line-throwing guns, rockets, and equipment almost enough to fit out a cruiser.

In short, an extremely expensive organization to run and one demanding constant care and supervision.

There are the deep-sea rescue tugs, their sizes, their power, their construction, and the job they do, and how they do it, whether it be towing or rescue.

There, too, are the men who man them. They are not immortal, they are not supermen—indeed, at times they are extremely human with all the human failings.

However, even when they fail, which is not often, they fail gloriously and gallantly.

They, of all the men who go down to the sea in ships, see the works of the Lord, and His wonders in the deep.

They see, too, tragedy—and occasionally humour.

Truly could they write on the bulkhead of their ships the prayer the Breton fishermen have on theirs: "You are so mighty and my ship is so small. Have mercy."

Whether they sail on the black-hulled blue and black funnelled Dutch tugs, the black and white *Abeilles* or the buff and black tugs of Overseas Towage and Salvage—or any other house flag under any ensign—they are grand men in grand ships.

Salute, rescue tugs! Salute, *Turmoil*!

MEMOIR

CAPTAIN DANIEL PARKER—Dan Parker of *Turmoil*—is dead.

But, through the pages of this book he is alive, as he was alive when it was being written. In fact the final proofs would have been waiting for him at the end of the voyage he never completed.

Turmoil was steaming through Dover Straits on the evening of 8th of August, 1955, when Parker slipped, fell from the bridge and was severely injured. Chief Officer Gavin Lindsay radioed ashore for medical assistance and a motor boat, with doctor on board, raced out to her, took Parker and raced back ashore.

But Parker died as it drew alongside the pier.

Thus half his promise to himself—half of the challenge he had thrown to the sea—was fulfilled. Nay, more than half, because Dan had his funeral service in a little grey Hampshire church, with flowers.

His ashes alone were scattered on the Solent and somehow I think Dan would consider that complete victory. I can almost see his slow, thin smile and can hear him say: "These, the cold grey ashes I will concede you. I had my funeral ashore, with the organ pealing slow music—and there were flowers."

I came to know of that challenge in an odd way.

Parker disliked publicity. He even hated it, and when his name and that of *Turmoil's* rang around the world after his brave effort to save *Flying Enterprise* he retreated even farther into that haven of reserve behind which few people ever penetrated.

When I undertook to write the broader story of *Turmoil* I received a wealth of willing co-operation from nearly everyone concerned—except Dan Parker. I wrote to him and in reply came a short letter.

"Enough has been written. There is nothing I can add."

There was but one thing to do and that was to meet the man on the ship, meet Parker and *Turmoil* together.

I did just that but even then co-operation was as far away as ever. It came as an incidental.

I joined *Turmoil* on her station, Cobh, near Cork, on a wild day with the wind screaming across the sky with promise of more to come. *Turmoil's* radio operators were dealing with a whole string of calls for assistance ranging from ships off the Azores to a liner driving ashore in Plymouth Sound.

Turmoil went to "Stand-by"—which meant being ready to go in ten seconds flat.

Parker and I stood together on the small bridge and talked of this and that through that wild morning until the first glint of grey dawn.

Out of nothing he suddenly said: "Why do you want to write about me and *Turmoil*? There's been far too much written already." His bleak, blue eyes probed at me coldly.

I produced my reasons and watched them bounce off him like hailstones off a roof. I was getting nowhere fast.

Then a coaster let out a soulful yelp around the corner. The sea was beating it unmercifully and it wanted help, and wanted it in large portions.

We picked up the conversation twenty-four hours later when the coaster had reached safety under its own steam without even a "thank you" to *Turmoil* for standing by.

I commented on its ingratitude and Dan shrugged it off. "Perhaps it made him feel better knowing we were around. What other reasons can you show for wanting to write about me and *Turmoil*?"

We had taken the full round turn. I had been awake for more than twenty-four hours and Dan had nearly doubled that. Once more the hailstones bounced.

Arising from nothing I remarked that the coaster had darn few places to which to run with the wind in that quarter and her with her screw out of the water two thirds of the time. The Devon coast along its north line offers nothing and battling into Milford Haven, with a westerly wind wiping its eye, can be hell.

Dan sat up and took notice.

Did I know that stretch?

Did I? I'd sailed it boy and man in most sorts of ships from schooners, yachts, coasters, big tramps and in mine-sweepers. I had mineswept from Milford Haven with the sea throwing the sweep over the quarter with St. Anne's Head looming over us like a cloud.

"You know Milford Haven?" says Dan.

We talked of this and that. We found we had served under the same senior officers, we found we had hammered at the same stubborn minefield, we found we had sailed on the same "milk run" convoy route.

That night, with *Turmoil* lifting and falling uneasily along-side the Deep Water Quay at Cobh, she being at "immediate notice for steam", which means ready to go at the drop of a hat—I got to know Dan Parker.

He talked to me of the yachts he had commanded, he talked to me of his family, he showed me photographs, little treasured snapshots. He kept them in a drawer full of pictures of *Flying Enterprise*, *World Concord* and other rescues, but the family pictures were on top.

After a sleep we woke to find a watery sun showing and Parker and I went for a walk into the rain-drenched hills behind Cobh, never farther away than the sound of her recalling siren could reach.

We leaned over a gate looking at the good, wet earth, at the fields green and fresh, at the trees showing a first touch of life.

Dan tapped me on the chest and his chilly blue eyes shipped a twinkle and a shade of warmth.

"You came near to writing something sensible once when you took two of your characters off their ships and walked 'em into the country where there was not a ship in sight nor a strip of sea to be seen."

I blinked. It was the first time he had admitted ever having read anything I had written.

"I liked that bit in *Proud Waters*," he said. "I read it two or three times and I still go back to that bit."

No critic can ever produce in me a brighter glow.

And then he talked.

"I never liked the sea. Like you, I was frightened by it when I was a kid and alone on deck at night on my father's sailing trawler. And I never forgave it. As I grew older I learned to respect it and its power, but it never made me cringe. I've always fought it.

"When things were tough I used to say to it: 'Do your damnedest but I'll be buried ashore—with flowers.' I used to say it to my crews when things were going hard—how hard you know. And when it was all over they would shout, 'No flowers yet, sir?' "

It became a litany with him.

It became part of a dream he had to wind up ashore with a little shop, a shelf or two of cigarettes, perhaps some stamps and a room behind the shop with the family in it. And behind the room a piece of garden.

He came near to getting it, too, when the tumult and shouting died and the smoke thinned and blew away in 1945.

But the sea reached out and called him back.

He went on fighting it, this time in rescue tugs. He became Parker of *Turmoil* when all he wanted was to be Parker of the little shop.

He met defeat more than once. And grieved, privately. He had success and won. And when he won he exulted, privately, because that was his way.

When we returned on board he almost shyly showed me a spindly, wispy little plant in a pot. He was battling heroically to keep it alive—a losing battle.

"The damn' sea is killing it, as it always kills everything— or nearly everything," he said.

Tenderly he picked a dried leaf from its stem.

"But I'm not beaten yet. I'm going to take it home next leave and plant it in the earth ashore."

He shifted the little plant so that it got some of the pale, yellow sunshine.

"And it won't get me, either. When I go I'm going to have a church service ashore—with flowers."

Dan had his wish. To all intents and purposes he was ashore when he died. He had the church service, he had the flowers. All that the sea had was a handful of grey ashes.

You won, Dan, won handsomely.

EWART BROOKES.

Mullion Cove,
Cornwall.